The Eschatology Handbook

The Bible Speaks to Us Today About Endtimes

Val J. Sauer

John Knox Press
ATLANTA

Library of Congress Cataloging in Publication Data
Sauer, Val J., 1938-
    The eschatology handbook.

    Bibliography: p.
    1. Eschatology—Biblical teaching. I. Title.
BS680.E8S28   236   81-82348
ISBN 0-8042-0066-1 (pbk.)   AACR2

© copyright John Knox Press 1981
10 9 8 7 6 5 4 3 2 1
Printed in the United States of America
John Knox Press
Atlanta, Georgia 30365

To my wife Connie, for her words of encouragement, her self-giving attitude during the many hours of preparation and study, and for being a loving and helpful partner in our Christian pilgrimage, I dedicate this work.

Acknowledgments

Those who read this book will see that I owe much to the work of others, and I have given credit to them in places where it is due. If I failed to give credit where credit was due it was unintentional and I apologize for the oversight. In all cases I tried to present the viewpoint of others as fairly and as accurately as possible.

I wish to extend my appreciation to Dr. Bernard Ramm for his helpful suggestions and his guidance in working through many materials relating to eschatology. His words of encouragement provided the needed incentive to overcome some difficult problems. I also want to thank Dr. Manfred Brauch for his observations and comments relating to the format of this material. A special thanks is in order for Dr. Myron Chartier for providing suggestions in formulating the study questions. A special word of thanks is also in order for Vicki Miller and the editorial staff of John Knox Press for their helpful suggestions. And finally, a special thank-you to Mrs. Kaehl Volesky for typing and proofreading this manuscript.

There have been many others too numerous to mention that have provided encouragement in the preparation of this study; their help and encouragement is greatly appreciated.

Introduction

There have always been differences of opinion regarding some of the basic teachings of the Christian faith. But in no area have diversities been so many as in the area of biblical prophecy, especially those prophecies which point to events still in the future. Some differences are primary, others are minor. Some color all of one's theological thinking, others can be filed in small compartments. For example, there are three different schools of thought regarding the millennium, and three views of the tribulation rapture. The view one finally takes on these subjects will have an overriding influence on his outlook on world events, and his understanding of the events relating to the return of our Lord.

The purpose of this study is to provide the Christian layperson with an introduction to a biblical view of final things. This study is not designed for the casual reader, but for the person who wants to do some serious thinking and Bible study about the Bible's teaching of final things. The underlying theme is that an understanding of biblical eschatology can provide the Christian believer with a view of history and the assurance of its final conclusion, can assure the Christian of an ultimate destiny, and can correct wrong emphasis.

Faced with the possibility of an atomic war, the reality of death, and the threat of ecological disaster, biblical eschatology assures the Christian that a loving God has not abandoned his creation. Creation and redemption, the beginning and end of history, are acts of God. Biblical eschatology declares that history is moving toward an ultimate goal, the redemption of creation. Furthermore, the Christian is assured of his ultimate destiny and that destiny is to have eternal fellowship with God. Along with this assurance, an understanding of biblical eschatology provides the believer with a glimpse of the nature of that destiny. Many popular books have appeared that discuss biblical eschatology. Common to these many books are fanciful speculations and conclusions based on questionable biblical interpretations. Biblical eschatology is an integral part of Christian theology, and an understanding of biblical eschatology can provide the Christian believer with a balanced view of Christian doctrine.

This study guide has two main parts. Part I deals with ideas and concepts that are basic in any study of biblical eschatology. First, the book defines biblical eschatology, and then describes why it is important to have an understanding of biblical eschatology. Second, the book describes several viewpoints that have been put forth in interpreting passages in the Bible relating to eschatology. There have been Christians, and there are Christians who love the Lord Jesus Christ, yet have different views on biblical eschatology. Third, an understanding of biblical eschatology is discussed.

Part II of this guide discusses certain events of biblical eschatology. These events include death, the intermediate state, the second coming of Jesus, the millennium, the resurrection, and eternal destiny. This guide avoids speculation and sensationalism and speaks only about what God has spoken to us recorded in Scripture. It also recognizes the fact that God has spoken in language, symbols, and concepts comprehensible to the human mind.

I believe that I have developed a guide to a balanced biblical view of eschatology. This guide can be used on an individual basis or within the context of a Bible study class, a Sunday school class, or some other group experience. The study section at the back of the book can be used to initiate discussion, to test the reader's understanding of what he or she has read, and to help the serious reader dig deeper. Questions on each chapter, a selected bibliography, a glossary of terms, and notes are included.

I strongly encourage each person using this study guide to check out the Scripture passages under discussion. I also encourage the use of Bible commentaries and Bible dictionaries as well as other reference materials (footnotes in some Bibles only represent a viewpoint that may or may not be consistent with what the biblical text actually states).

Val J. Sauer Jr.
Watertown, South Dakota

Table of Contents

\

Part II

EVENTS IN A
BIBLICAL ESCHATOLOGY

RESOURCES
FOR
STUDY

PART I

ESTABLISHING A FOUNDATION FOR A BIBLICAL ESCHATOLOGY

§

CHAPTER 1

The Meaning and Necessity of Eschatology

The term "eschatology" does not appear in the Bible. It is a word derived from two Greek words, *eschatos* and *logia.* The word *eschatos* has the meaning "last"; it conveys the sense of extreme, that which is last in place or time. The word *logia* is derived from the word *logos* which conveys the sense of a discourse or saying. When used with *eschatos, logia* has the meaning of a teaching, or a discussion of that which is last in place or time. Thus, eschatology can be defined as the doctrine or teaching of last things.

Biblical eschatology deals with God's final acts toward his creation, the last days, the promise of the future, and the hope which grows out of this promise. Scripture focuses on Jesus Christ's coming as the consummation of the last things. Biblical eschatology is grounded in what God has done in the death and resurrection of Jesus Christ and looks forward to the time of consummation in the return of Christ. Biblical eschatology speaks primarily of the anticipation of Jesus Christ who has already been revealed and who will "appear a second time . . . to save those who are eagerly waiting for him" (Heb. 9:28).

How does eschatology relate to our Christian faith? Does

eschatology have anything to say about our world and its problems? Will biblical eschatology help Christians understand their Christian faith and their future destiny? An understanding of biblical eschatology can provide the Christian with a view of history, the assurance of its final conclusion, and assure the Christian of his ultimate destiny.

The Necessity of Eschatology

An eschatology certainly is necessary. In our technological age people are taking a long look at future prospects. There are many persons who believe that detailed studies of the future are a vital necessity. If we are to guarantee our survival the future must become calculable.

The threat of a global, push-button atomic war poses the possibility that millions of people may be killed with no warning. Thousands of people die each year from cancer, heart disease, emphysema, as well as from many other causes. Some twelve thousand people alone die each day from starvation. For many death has become an undesirable but necessary by-product of a technological society.

Our environmental exploitation has taken on apocalyptic dimensions. This is illustrated by two examples: (1) Our rapidly increasing consumption of carbon-based fuels (oil, coal, gas) releases an increasing amount of carbon dioxide into the earth's atmosphere. When nature's cycles can no longer balance the equation, by using up carbon dioxide in plants and releasing a corresponding amount of oxygen, the remaining carbon dioxide forms a layer in the atmosphere. This layer, or "roof," will let the sun's rays through, but will prevent the heat from escaping. Adding to this thermal pollution, i.e., energy input into earth's atmosphere, the earth's atmosphere could be warmed by more than two degrees centigrade within a hundred years. The consequences of this warming action would melt the ice caps and the sea level would rise by three to four hundred feet. While this temperature rise may seem insignificant, it is only necessary to remember that Holland is now below sea level protected only by dykes, and that most of America's East

Coast and Gulf Coast, including Florida, is below the 400 foot mark.

(2) It has been estimated that 146 million tons of man-made aerial garbage are spewed into the United State's atmosphere each year. One of these pollutants is sulfur dioxide, which, when combined with moisture, forms a sulfuric acid mist that can burn deep into the lungs. Other pollutants include such things as carbon monoxide (colorless, odorless, but potentially deadly), benzopyrene (which has given cancer to mice), acrolein (an ingredient in tear gas), peroxyacyle nitrate (a cause of the sore chests, burning eyes, and coughing that afflicts many people on smoggy days), and countless tiny specks of lead, asbestos, carbon, ash, oil, and grease. Lakes, rivers, and streams have been receptacles for refuse. Tons of raw sewage, animal and vegetable waste, and pulp have been discharged into the water supply by community sewage disposal systems, packing plants and canneries, factories and steel mills.

The fear of a nuclear war, the reality of death, and the threat of ecological suicide seem to indicate that there is little hope for man's survival. At this point a biblical eschatology can proclaim hope for the Christian by providing him with a view of history. The Bible teaches that creation and consummation, the beginning and end of history, are acts of God. The Bible proclaims that history has a beginning and that it moves toward an ultimate goal. That goal is God's redemption of creation.

Confronted with the reality of death, an understanding of biblical eschatology can assure the Christian of his ultimate destiny. Man was created in the "image of God" (Gen. 1:26-30) for a purpose—to be God's representative in the world exercising authority over creation. Created in the "image of God" man has the capacity for responsible relationship with God as well as in living responsibly with his fellowmen. When sin destroyed the relationship between God and man (Gen. 3), God set into motion his plan for the redemption of mankind and the ultimate destruction of sin. Biblical eschatology speaks of God's plan of salvation centering in the person and and work of Jesus Christ (John 3:16). The Bible's teaching of last things assures the Christian of his ultimate destiny and provides him with a glimpse of that destiny.

A number of books and films have appeared that discuss biblical eschatology. These books and films seem to indicate an increasing interest on the part of many persons to know what the future holds for mankind. In many instances these books and films see eschatology as something happening totally in the future rather than understanding it as an integral part of Christian teaching. An understanding of biblical eschatology can provide a balanced Christian perspective. This can be accomplished by understanding events of eschatology not as speculations about the end of the world, but rather as the completion of our salvation begun in this life.

The Nature of Apocalyptic

One aspect of biblical eschatology is its apocalyptic character. Apocalypticism has to do with the unveiling or revealing of that which is unknown. The use of signs, symbols, and images by the biblical writers is an attempt to describe that which has not been seen or experienced. It is an attempt to describe the indescribable. In order to better understand biblical eschatology it will be necessary to briefly discuss the nature of apocalyptic. The reason for this brief discussion of apocalyptic is that many of the biblical symbols for understanding God's acts of salvation are apocalyptic symbols.

The term "apocalyptic" is derived from the Greek word *apocalypsis* (Rev. 1:1), which means "revelation or disclosure." Apocalyptic is a term used to describe a certain type of literature that is believed to contain revelations of heavenly secrets or events which describe the end of the world and the inauguration of the kingdom of God. In order to gain a broader understanding of apocalyptic thought, a brief look at its historical background is necessary.

Hebrew prophecy survived the fall of Jerusalem in 587 B.C. and continued into the post-exilic era. In this period we see the emergence of men like Haggai, Zechariah, Obadiah, Malachi, Joel as well as many other unnamed prophets. However, during the post-exilic era a belief gradually developed which saw the emphasis of prophecy diminish with reference to the pre-exilic prophetic message (Zech. 13:2–6).

There are several reasons that help explain the decline in Hebrew prophecy. First, from the time of Ezra onwards there was an increasing emphasis on the Law. The teaching of the Law by the scribes began to replace the preaching by the "inspired prophets." Second, the prophetic message was directed toward the purification of the Temple ritual. Its purpose was the enrichment of the formal worship of God. A third reason for the decline of Hebrew prophecy was to be found in the influence of foreign culture which contained elements hostile to Jewish religious heritage. Many false prophets, by their unbridled feelings, wild dances, and bodily lacerations, cast a dark shadow on prophecy in the minds of many who knew of the idolatries of Babylon. Fourth, there were many irresponsible prophets whose utterances could readily lend themselves to those seeking political agitation. Thus, in the course of time the voice of prophecy was stilled.

Israel had returned to the land and was faithful to the Law. According to the Jewish understanding of righteousness, the conditions laid down by the prophets were satisfied, but the kingdom did not come. What came was unprecedented suffering. Antiochus Epiphanes (168 B.C.) attempted to destroy the Jewish faith. An image of a pagan deity, perhaps in the likeness of Antiochus, was set up upon the Temple altar. The Jews popularly spoke of this as the "Abomination of Desolation."

> Greek soldiers and their paramours performed licentious heathen rites in the very Temple courts. Swine were sacrificed on the altar. The drunken orgy associated with the worship of Bacchus was made compulsory. Conversely, Jews were forbidden, under penalty of death, to practice circumcision, Sabbath observance, or the observance of the feasts of the Jewish year. Copies of the Hebrew Scriptures were ordered destroyed.[1]

Those who resisted were tortured and put to death. The religious and political liberty won by the Maccabean rebellion did not bring in the kingdom of God. Instead of God's rule came the rule of secular, worldly Hasmoneans followed in 63 B.C. by Roman rule. Instead of peace and prosperity Israel met suffering and political bondage.

No prophet appeared to announce "Thus says the Lord" and to interpret to the people of God the suffering inflicted upon them. However, a new voice began to be heard that did speak concerning the sufferings of the righteous and the delay of the kingdom of God. This new voice we would call "apocalyptic." Its basic message was that what the prophets had foretold and promised was now at the point of being realized. The apocalyptists taught that God was going to intervene in history in a unique way to bring salvation to the righteous and judgment to the wicked. Apocalyptic literature is a literature of hope directed to a people in despair. It was not written to be a puzzle for the curious but to be a source of strength to people in a situation that was for them a supreme moment of destiny. Apocalyptic literature is literature for hard times.

Apocalyptic is not to be seen as a substitute for prophecy. The origin of apocalyptic is to be found in Hebrew prophecy whose thought and language provided the basis from which later apocalyptic writings were to appear. Such passages as Ezekiel 38—39, Zechariah 1—8 and 9—14, Joel 3, and Isaiah 24—27 contain the seeds from which apocalyptic is developed.

Apocalyptic then can be understood as the continuation, or in a sense, the development of prophecy with a new form, feeling, and content. The difference between the prophet and the apocalyptist can be stated in the following way: the prophets foretold the future that would arise out of the present, while the apocalyptists foretold the future that would break into the present. The message of the apocalyptists touches base with the prophetic message to meet the needs and hopes of God's people in difficult circumstances. The message of the apocalyptists was a response of faith to the difficult times for the purpose of encouraging and strengthening the faith of God's people.

There are certain characteristics that distinguish apocalyptic from other kinds of literature.[2] First, apocalyptic is a type of literature which claims to be revelations or disclosures of divine secrets made known to certain persons. God did not speak to the apocalyptists by his Spirit as he had to the prophets. The solutions to the problem of evil and the coming of God's kingdom were revealed through dreams, visions, or heavenly journeys with angelic guides.

Second, the prophet was commanded by God to declare the message given to him by word of mouth which later was put in writing by the prophet or his followers. The apocalyptist, on the other hand, was told to put his message in written form so that the faithful among God's people could read it. God's command to the prophet was, "You shall speak to them this word" (Jer. 13:12). His word to the apocalyptist was, "Write what you see in a book" (Rev. 1:11). From the beginning of the second century B.C. divine revelation had come to be associated with the written word rather than the spoken word. It seemed only fitting that fresh revelations should also appear in written form.

A third characteristic of apocalyptic literature is its extensive use of symbolism. The apocalyptists had the difficult task of interpreting the inexpressible nature of their dreams and visions. As the language of common prose seemed to be inadequate for this task the apocalyptists used the imaginative language of poetry as the medium to express their experiences. Apocalyptic literature abounds in the use of the beasts and animals, seals, in rivers and mountains and stars, and in personages both celestial and infernal. Generally speaking, we can say that men and nations are symbolized by animals or beasts, good angels are symbolized by men, and fallen angels by stars. Sometimes the meaning is uncertain.

> The apocalyptists did not always (or even usually) think it necessary to explain their symbolism. There appear to have been times when it would have been politically unwise for them to have done so. They evidently trusted that their friends would be able to discern their essential meaning, and that their enemies would not be able to do so. Part of their reason for using bizarre symbolism will also be that they were trying to describe something that was too big for words. After all, their main theme was the end of the world, and this is something for which we have no adequate language.[3]

A fourth characteristic of apocalyptic literature is its pseudonymity. Many apocalyptists attributed their writings to some Old Testament saints in order to validate their message.[4] This was not an attempt by the apocalyptists to deceive their readers. Rather the apocalyptist was trying to express what he thought the Old Testament saint, in whose name he wrote, would have said had he been living in the time in which the apocalyptist was living. Examples of these writings and their approximate date of composition are:

a. 1 Enoch (from 164 B.C. onwards)
b. The Testaments of the XII Patriarchs (latter part of second century B.C.)
c. The Psalms of Solomon (48 B.C.)
d. The Assumption of Moses (A.D. 6-30)
e. The Martyrdom of Isaiah (no date given)
f. The Life of Adam and Eve or The Apocalypse of Moses (shortly before A.D. 70)
g. The Apocalypse of Abraham 9—32 (A.D. 70-100)
h. The Testament of Abraham (first century A.D.)
i. 2 Enoch or the Book of the Secrets of Enoch (first century A.D.)

Apocalyptic eschatology is a particular kind of eschatology embodying certain distinctive characteristics which are developments of prophetic religion.[5] First, *dualism* is a concept that stresses the contrast between the present age and the coming age. The present age is characterized by evil; the coming age will see an end to suffering, violence, and evil. The transition from the present age to the coming age can be accomplished only by a visitation of God, a supernatural inbreaking into history. This dualism is historical and temporal, not metaphysical or cosmic.

Second, *determinism* is the idea that the course of this evil age is predetermined and must run its course. The kingdom must await its appointed time. This idea has often led to the dividing of time into a series of predetermined periods by which the time of the end could be calculated.

A third characteristic is *pessimism*. While the apocalyptists never lost confidence that God would finally triumph and bring in his kingdom, nevertheless they were pessimistic about the present age. The problem of the suffering of the righteous had led to the conclusion that God had withdrawn his help from the righteous in the present age and that salvation could be expected only in the coming age.

A fourth characteristic is *ethical passivity*. The apocalyptists did not announce God's judgments on his people. Their problem was that there is a righteous remnant which is overwhelmed by undeserved evil. Therefore, there is very little ethical exhortation in the apocalyptic writings. (*The Testament of the XII Patriarchs* would be an exception.)

A distinction must be drawn between biblical and non-biblical apocalyptic. The characteristics listed above apply to non-biblical apocalyptic, but do not apply at all points with biblical apocalyptic. The New Testament religion is apocalyptic in that it shares a dualistic structure of the two ages while not being deterministic, pessimistic, or ethically passive. God's kingdom is not the product of history, it comes from without; nevertheless, it is working in history and will finally transform history.

The book of Revelation, while sharing certain apocalyptic traits, stands apart at other points. It is not a pseudonymous work but bears the name of the author who writes as a prophet. John does not share the pessimism of the apocalyptists who despaired of history and saw hope only in the coming age. God was working redemptively both in history and at the end of history. This is portrayed by the lion who is the slain lamb (Rev. 5:5-6). Furthermore, John possesses a sense of moral urgency rebuking a faithless church and demanding repentance to avoid the divine judgment (Rev. 2:5, 16, 21, 22; 3:19).

The apocalyptists were not systematic theologians. Their purpose was not to develop exact definitions of faith. They were poets and visionaries who expressed their convictions in terms of traditional imagery which was at times highly imaginary and often obscure. Their purpose was to express in simple language the inexpressible mysteries of God. They believed in God, and believed that he had some purpose for the world he created, and that he had the power to accomplish that purpose.

They believed that God was a loving God who was in control of history.

The doctrine of the Incarnation proclaims that God was active in human history in the person and work of Jesus Christ to achieve his great purpose of redeeming creation. The kingdom of God comes only by the power of God and that its blessings are reserved for those who "become children of God."

CHAPTER 2

Types of Eschatology

Throughout the history of the Christian church there have been attempts to interpret the eschatological statements in the Bible. Numerous interpretations have been suggested in an attempt to discern the meaning of what the Bible says about the endtime events. No interpretation has been totally right or totally wrong in its outlook on biblical eschatology. This writer's position is that of "inaugurated eschatology." I shall describe this viewpoint first, and then describe several other viewpoints. It is not my purpose to do an in-depth theological evaluation of differing viewpoints, but to describe several viewpoints other Bible interpreters have suggested. It is important to remember that there has never been only "one way" to interpret biblical eschatology, contrary to what many of the popular "bible prophecy experts" are proclaiming.

Inaugurated Eschatology

The viewpoint adopted in this book is that of "inaugurated eschatology." This interpretation seeks to maintain the necessary tension between the "realized eschatology" and the future dimension of the eschatological teaching of the New Testament. This tension can be seen in the gospel which sees Jesus not only coming to announce the kingdom of God, but to perform the decisive event through which God will inaugurate that kingdom. Jesus' life

> was a life wrought out in conscious obedience to the eschatological will of God, a life in which proclamation of the impending advent of the Reign of God and the performance of the signs which heralded its approach culminated in the suffering of the cross as the decisive event by which the eschatological process should be inaugurated.[1]

The death and resurrection of Jesus Christ is seen as the midpoint of the entire line of revelation and that from this midpoint the future takes on new meaning for the believer. This decisive event, the death and resurrection of Jesus, sets into motion the eschatological process—the coming of the reign of God and triumph of the Son of man. Yet at the same time, during Jesus' earthly ministry, the kingdom is dawning, though it has not yet come. Basic to inaugurated eschatology is the concept of the kingdom of God.

Jesus began his ministry with these words, "The time is fulfilled, and the kingdom of God is at hand; repent, and believe in the gospel" (Mark 1:15). The implication of Jesus' message is that men are living in a unique moment in history, and that God is initiating a new age in the history of his dealings with them. The coming of the kingdom of God is not man's work, but God's deed. In the person and work of Jesus, the kingdom of God has broken into the world. What the prophets had promised has now become a reality.

There seems to be no doubt in Jesus' mind that in his ministry God's kingdom has arrived. "But if it is by the finger of God that I cast out demons, then the kingdom of God has come upon you" (Luke 11:20). At times, Jesus unmistakably sounds the note of fulfillment:

> Blessed are the eyes which see what you see! For I tell you that many prophets and kings desired to see what you see, and did not see it, and to hear what you hear, and did not hear it.
> (Luke 10:23-24)

> Go and tell John what you have seen and heard: the blind receive their sight, the lame walk, lepers are cleansed, and the

> deaf hear, the dead are raised up, the poor have good news
> preached to them. And blessed is he who takes no offense at me.
>
> (Luke 7:22–23)

While Jesus refused to give signs upon demand to authenticate his ministry (Mark 8:12; Matt. 4:1–11; Luke 11:29), as we see in his reply to John the Baptist's question, Jesus did regard his mighty works as signs of the presence of the kingdom. The miracles of Jesus were the kingdom of God in action. The message of the New Testament is that the One who will bring in the kingdom of God in the future has appeared in the present in Jesus himself, and in him the powers of the coming age are already at work. Thus Jesus can proclaim the kingdom of God with a unique authority and can challenge men for a decision concerning this kingdom.

But Jesus also saw a future coming of the kingdom of God. In three passages Jesus speaks of the day when God's kingdom will be revealed in power and glory. The first passage is Luke 17:26–30:

> As it was in the days of Noah, so will it be in the days of the Son of man. They ate, they drank, they married, they were given in marriage, until the day when Noah entered the ark, and the flood came and destroyed them all. Likewise as it was in the days of Lot—they ate, they drank, they bought, they sold, they planted, they built, but on the day when Lot went out from Sodom fire and brimstone rained from heaven and destroyed them all—so will it be on the day when the Son of man is revealed.

This passage depicts the revelation of the Son of man against the background of the end of the existing order. The appearance of the Son of man will be a "surprise to the godless world." It will be an event that will take place without any preceding or definite indications of its day or hour. Life in this age will continue as it has in the past until the appearance of the Son of man. This appearance will interrupt the corrupt processes of this age.

The second passage pictures the breakdown of the universe when the Son of man comes:

> But in those days, after that tribulation, the sun will be darkened, and the moon will not give its light, and the stars will be falling from heaven, and the powers in the heavens will be shaken. And then they will see the Son of man coming in clouds with great power and glory.
>
> (Mark 13:24-26)

In language drawn from the prophets (Isaiah 13:10; 34:4; Daniel 7:13ff; Ezekiel 32ff; Joel 2:10) Jesus depicts the familiar accompaniments of the day of the Lord. G. R. Beasley-Murray understands this cosmic confusion as a preparation for the introduction of the glory and coming salvation of the Son of man. He states:

> Before his appearing the heavenly bodies lose their brilliance and become dark, so that the revelation of the glory of the Son fills the cosmos. It is the sole object of vision in heaven and on earth. When God steps forth for salvation the universe pales before him.[2]

While the language of this passage may sound strange in an atomic age, nevertheless it seems to have a semblance of sober truth and grim reality. It would be unscientific, to say the least, to state that these words may not refer to objective phenomena in the form of cosmic disturbances prior to the return of Christ.

The third passage has its setting in another world, for surely it is not in our space time world that the dead, as well as the living, will stand before the Son of man:

> When the Son of man comes in his glory, and all the angels with him, then he will sit on his glorious throne. Before him will be gathered all the nations, and he will separate them one from another as a shepherd separates the sheep from the goats.
>
> (Matt. 25:31-32)

These verses are part of a prophetic picture of the final judgment awaiting all people. The Son of man returns with divine power and acting for God executes the final judgment of all mankind.

These passages express the unimaginable in human symbols, but taken together, these sayings of Jesus give divine assurance that there will be a future coming of Christ in history. It is the event which we call the consummation of the kingdom of God.

However, between the present reality of the kingdom of God and its future coming in power and glory stands the cross. Towards the end of his ministry Jesus said, "For the Son of man also came not to be served but to serve, and to give his life as a ransom for many" (Mark 10:45). Jesus saw his life, and ultimately his death as the final act of obedience which crowns his work as Suffering Servant. It is the last and bitterest battle with the powers of evil that would usher in the "new age."

In the life, death, and resurrection of Jesus the new age was inaugurated. In a real sense the future has become present, salvation is realized, and Christians can enjoy God's kingdom. Already they possess the Holy Spirit promised by the prophets for the last times. But the coming day of God's final victory in Christ, the parousia, is sure. The hope of the final victory is so much the more vivid because of the unshakably firm conviction that the battle that decides the victory has already taken place. The hope for the Christian lies in God's final consummation when "Christ who is our life appears" (Col. 3:4). This hope is no private bliss of souls in the beyond, but the fulfillment of each individual human life in its personal destiny.

The viewpoint of eschatology that sees elements of truth in "realized eschatology" but also looks for eschatological events in the future is that of "inaugurated eschatology."

Consistent Eschatology

A second way of interpreting the Bible's teaching about last things is through the viewpoint of "consistent eschatology." From New Testament times until the beginning of the twentieth century, there have been periods of time in which the Christian message lost its eschatological force because the death and resurrection of Jesus Christ ceased to be at the center of the gospel. One such period of time was the late nineteenth and early twentieth century. For many theologians

Jesus was seen only as a prophet who taught the eternal ideals of the fatherhood of God, the brotherhood of all men, the infinite value of the soul, and the ethics of love. The eschatology of the New Testament was seen as the dispensable wrapping in which the Jesus of history was encased. To get at the truth of the gospel the eschatological wrapping had to be stripped away and discarded. Jesus was reduced to an ethical teacher compatible with popular ideas.

This idealized picture of Jesus was destroyed by the work of Albert Schweitzer. In his book, *The Quest of the Historical Jesus*, Schweitzer maintains that Jesus' eschatology is the key to understanding his life. In fact, Schweitzer argues, it is only by a consistent application of the eschatological category that we can understand Jesus at all, hence "consistent eschatology."

Albert Schweitzer believed that Jesus' mission was to proclaim the approaching eschatological climax. God's judgment was about to fall, the end of the world was about to come, and human history was going to end in some great catastrophic event. Jesus saw himself as the one to take upon himself the burden and offer himself as the ransom which would enable God to bring in the new age. With one purpose in mind, Jesus went up to Jerusalem to die in order that history might end and God's great act of consummation might take place.

But the great act of consummation did not take place. History did not end. The kingdom did not come. God did not act. Jesus died upon the cross with a cry of frustration and despair, "My God, my God, why hast thou forsaken me?" (Matt. 27:46). Concerning Jesus, Albert Schweitzer writes,

> In the knowledge that He is the coming Son of Man [Jesus] lays hold of the wheel of the world to set it moving on that last revolution which is to bring all ordinary history to a close. It refuses to turn, and He throws Himself upon it. Then it does turn; and crushes Him. Instead of bringing in the eschatological conditions, He has destroyed them. The wheel rolls onward, and the mangled body of the one immeasurably great Man, who was strong enough to think of Himself as the spiritual ruler of mankind and to bend history to His purpose, is hanging upon it still. That is His victory and His reign.[3]

For Albert Schweitzer Jesus was a deluded Jewish fanatic who died as a martyr to his own delusion. Jesus was the man who lived and taught in Palestine, but he is of little help to modern man. His ideas were alien to modern concepts of history. There are not many followers of consistent eschatology today. One reason may be that for many conservatives this viewpoint of eschatology is not close enough to the biblical witness, while some liberals would find secular philosophies more satisfying. A major weakness of consistent eschatology is that it fails to show how Christianity could have survived if it began and developed only through disappointments, and what it was that gave the Christians strength to maintain their faith through all persecutions. The positive emphasis of consistent eschatology is the fact that Jesus must be seen in light of his preaching and that there exists in the New Testament, in the preaching of Jesus, an eschatological tension and expectation. Furthermore, it is not possible to present the kingdom of God, from Jesus' preaching, wholly in terms of imminent, this-worldly categories.

Realized Eschatology

Another way of interpreting eschatology is described as "realized eschatology." In the letters of Paul and in the book of Acts the kingdom of God is seen as something which is very much in power already. God has confronted mankind in Jesus Christ. The kingdom has come in power and glory. In his book, *The Parables of the Kingdom,* C. H. Dodd states that much of Jesus' teachings indicate that Jesus was not greatly concerned about the future but rather in what God is doing now. Dodd believes that in Jesus the coming of the kingdom of God was shifted from the future to the present, hence the phrase "realized eschatology."

In what sense did Jesus declare that the kingdom of God was present? John the Baptist, while in prison, sent his disciples to Jesus to ask him if he was the One who is to come. Jesus' answer to John was, "The blind receive their sight and the lame walk, lepers are cleansed and the deaf hear, and the

dead are raised up, and the poor have good news preached to
them" (Matt. 11:5). In Jesus' ministry divine power was released in effective conflict with evil. Jesus himself declared,
"But if it is by the Spirit of God that I cast out demons, then
the kingdom of God has come upon you" (Matt. 12:28). Dodd
concludes that in Jesus' ministry eschatology has become realized.

> Here then is the fixed point from which our interpretation of
> the teaching regarding the Kingdom of God must start. It rep-
> resents the ministry of Jesus as "realized eschatology," that is
> to say, as the impact upon this world of the "powers of the
> world to come" in a series of events, unprecedented and un-
> repeatable, now in actual process.[4]

The basic affirmation of realized eschatology is that the
decisive event of the Jewish eschatological hope, the coming of
the kingdom of God, was regarded by Jesus as taking place
once and for all in his own ministry. It is true that Jesus used
the traditional apocalyptic symbolism, but he did this only to
indicate the "other-wordly" or absolute character of the kingdom of God. On the other hand, Jesus used the parables to illustrate and enforce the idea that the kingdom of God had
come upon men there and then. In "realized eschatology"
there are no future events. Everything has already happened.

If everything has already happened, then there can be no
place for the prophecies about the parousia in the teaching of
Jesus. Any teaching attributed to Jesus in the Gospels about
the parousia (i.e., Mark 13; Matt. 24; Luke 21: 5–28) are either
misunderstandings of Jesus' teaching or additions to Jesus'
teaching by the church. There will be no literal second coming
of Jesus Christ in history. Those passages which seem to speak
of a second coming are to be understood not in a literal sense
but in a way consistent with the concept of realized eschatology. The promise of a second coming is fulfilled in the coming of the Holy Spirit, in the life of the church (John 14:16–19;
16:12–16). Dodd believes that the final coming of Christ can
best be understood as occurring in the celebration of the
Eucharist.

At each Eucharist we are *there*—we are in the night in which He was betrayed, at Golgotha, before the empty tomb on Easter day, and in the upper room where He appeared; *and* we are at the moment of His coming, with angels and archangels and all the company of heaven, in the twinkling of an eye at the last trump.[5]

Realized eschatology provides a positive emphasis on the present aspect of the kingdom of God. God's victory was won, Christ had won it, and we have a share in this victory. The value of realized eschatology is its insistence that the present aspect of the kingdom of God must be located wholly in the life, death, and resurrection of Jesus Christ. Its principal weakness is that it must explain away a considerable amount of New Testament teaching which is inescapably future in its reference.

Idealized Eschatology

A fourth way of interpreting the Bible's teaching of end-times is from the viewpoint of "idealized eschatology." In this interpretation eschatology is not understood as a series of events at the end of history but as the fulfillment of the future in the present time. In other words what is experienced as death, or the end of a generation or period of time, is the end of history and the entrance of eternity into history.

The Christian hope is concerned with the future of every human being, the history of mankind, and the future of the natural world. In the viewpoint of idealized eschatology these three aspects taken together sum up Jesus' teaching concerning the kingdom of God.

The future of mankind. God deals with man in the tension between Law and gospel. Under the sign of Law, God places man in a state of responsibility that does not end even at death. God's judgment against sin is not fully revealed in history but points beyond history to a final judgment when God deals with sin. But under the sign of the gospel, God's love is revealed as a final and unbroken love. This love will not let the believer fall in death but will lead him beyond death into the glory of eternal life.

Men are called to new life in Christ (e.g., the Gospel according to St. John). However, the new life is "hid with Christ in God" (Col. 3:3), because the veil of sin still covers man in this earthly life. This contradiction calls for a solution which can only be realized by the death of our earthly existence through resurrection. The Christian faith sees man as a whole being. He sins as a whole being, he dies as a whole being, and he is raised to new life as a whole thing.

> To die means that God destroys totally the earthly form of person; to be resurrected means that God gives to the person a new, eternal form of being of body and soul. Thus the resurrection will be a transformation of the whole human being but will maintain at the same time the identity of the person and his history with God.[6]

The history of mankind. In faith we know that history moves towards its end because the very structure of history stands in opposition to the will of God. The history of mankind can be described by the laws of competition and the laws of struggle as well as the power of evil. Into this structure of history God places the church to enter into battle with human and superhuman powers to create a just order and to ease the hardships of the existence of mankind. But Christianity has not become master of the law of death, of evil, of the demonic in history.

In the viewpoint of idealized eschatology there is no progress in history toward the kingdom of God. The hope for history lies in the coming of Jesus Christ in glory. His coming will mean the end of history and the end of the meaning of history. The meaning of history is to be understood as that period of time in which God's purposes are worked out. In a very real sense Jesus' coming in glory is the end and the goal of history. Jesus' coming will also bring a judgment in which evil in the history of mankind will be revealed and the powers of evil will be rendered impotent. God's eternal kingdom will be the fulfillment and completion of the history of mankind.

The hope for the natural world. This natural world is the creation of God, but it is not his final work. In some strange way sin has even affected the natural laws of creation as seen in the struggle of life and death. God must free this natural world from the lowliness of creation and form it to correspond to the glory of his children. God will make an end to the world as we know it, but at the same time there will be a renewal and a completion of the world as it is now.

In idealized eschatology we are not to understand eschatology as a teaching of endtimes and events. To believe in a literal return of Christ, a literal coming of the kingdom of God, a literal judgment before Christ, etc., would mean that we are putting eschatology on the same level as matters of science and logic. Rather, eschatology has to do with this side of eternity and every generation is equally affected by eschatological events. The eschatological promises in the New Testament can become realities in our lives in the present time through faith.

Idealized eschatology rightly emphasizes the "depth-dimension" of salvation. In other words Christians receive the gift of eternal life through faith in Christ and in some sense experience the blessings of God's kingdom. However, this interpretation of eschatology does not do justice to those passages that speak of real events yet in the future in which history will be ended and eternity begins.

Dispensational Eschatology

Another approach to the interpretation of biblical eschatology is that taught in dispensationalism. This is the view popularized by Hal Lindsey in *The Late Great Planet Earth*, and in the notes of the *Scofield Reference Bible*. Dispensationalism is a system of biblical interpretation that "views the world as a household run by God."[7] In this view God is understood as "dispensing or administering" the affairs of the world according to his own will and in the various stages of revelation in the process of time. These various stages mark off the different economies, or dispensations in the unfolding of God's purpose. The sevenfold scheme of dispensations in dispensationalism are:[8]

1. The Dispensation of Innocency or Freedom (Genesis 1:28—3:6).

2. The Dispensation of Conscience or Self-Determination (Genesis 4:1—8:14).
3. The Dispensation of Civil Government (Genesis 8:15—11:9).
4. The Dispensation of Promise or Patriarchal Rule (Genesis 11:10—Exodus 18:27).
5. The Dispensation of the Mosaic Law (Exodus 18:28—Acts 1:26).
6. The Dispensation of Grace (Acts 2:1—Revelation 19:21).
7. The Dispensation of the Millennium (Revelation 20).

There are three essential marks or characteristics of dispensationalism: (1) Dispensationalism maintains a distinction between Israel and the church. Israel is understood in terms of the nation of Israel while the church is understood as the "Body of Christ." (2) Dispensationalism uses a system of Bible interpretation which is usually referred to as literal interpretation. The dispensational approach claims a consistent literal interpretation of the Scriptures.

> In other words, consistent literalism is the basis for dispensationalism, and since consistent literalism is the logical and obvious principle of interpretation, dispensationalism is more than justified.[9]

Dispensationalists believe that their system of biblical interpretation "is the only true Biblical view and is the one that harmonizes the whole body of revealed truth."[10] (3) Dispensationalism understands that the underlying purpose of God in the world is namely the manifestation of his own glory.

When we turn to dispensational eschatology, several prominent features stand out. First, dispensationalism claims that it is the only system that practices the literal principle of interpretation. Other systems of interpretation may practice literal interpretation at times, but not in every area of theology or on all parts of the Bible. "Consistent literalism is at the heart of dispensational eschatology."[11]

Second, dispensationalism teaches that there will be a literal fulfillment of Old Testament prophecies. If the prophecies of the Old Testament concerning the promise of the future made to Abraham and David are to be fulfilled, then there must be a period in which they will come to fulfillment. This period is the millennium. The purpose of the millennium is to fulfill God's oath and promise to David. It is the time when God will fulfill all of the prophecies of the Old Testament to Israel for their blessing.

> The Scriptures predict that there is coming a time when God will deal with the nation Israel again. This promise will be fulfilled in the coming millennial reign of Christ which will follow His return to the earth.[12]

Dispensationalism teaches that the church is in no way fulfilling these prophecies and that fulfillment of Israel's prophecies will occur in the millennium.

Third, a prominent feature of dispensationalism is the clear distinction between Israel and the church. Dispensationalism teaches that the church does not fulfill any of the prophecies in the Old Testament regarding Israel.

Fourth, dispensationalism teaches that the church will be taken from the earth before the beginning of the tribulation. This teaching is more commonly referred to as the pretribulation rapture of the church. Many dispensationalists believe that the blessed hope of the believer "is translation, not resurrection."[13] An important part of dispensational eschatology is the pretribulational rapture of the church.

Fifth, the doctrine of the millennial kingdom is an integral part of dispensational eschatology. Dispensationalists teach that God's promises to Israel will be literally fulfilled in the millennium. God's purposes for Israel will be realized when Israel dwells in the land of Palestine under the rule of the Son of David on a Davidic throne in Jerusalem. In the millennium Jesus Christ will reign on the throne of David over a political earthly kingdom. The future of Israel as a nation as well as a people involves the fulfillment of a literal kingdom on earth with Jesus Christ as king.

These are the principal features of dispensational eschatology. The positive influence of dispensationalism is to be seen in its emphasis on encouraging Bible study as well as an emphasis on the Christian hope in the coming of our Lord. The evangelistic thrust of some dispensationalists is to be commended. John Walvoord's book, *The Return of the Lord*, is cited as an example of dispensational teaching combined with an evangelistic emphasis.

There are, however, a number of weaknesses in the dispensational approach to eschatology. First, an extreme literalistic interpretation of Scripture seems to distort the meaning and intent of some prophetic passages. More important, however, is that "consistent literalism" tends to force all prophetic Scripture into a rigidly defined pattern. There is more to interpretation than discovering the meaning of words.

> Prophetic interpretation must proceed in the light of context, the mood of the author, the conditions to which he is writing, and the over-all pattern of the Scriptures. Not all prophetic Scripture can be interpreted literally.[14]

Several modes of human speech, i.e., metaphor, allegory, parable, symbol, etc., are used by the biblical writers in which God has set forth his truth. For example, such statements by Jesus as "I am the door" (John 10:9), or "I am the good Shepherd" (John 10:11), or ". . . unless you eat the flesh of the Son of man and drink his blood, you have no life in you" (John 6:53) if interpreted in a literalistic way would lead to some peculiar ideas. Jesus' statements as recorded in Matthew 5:29–30 should settle once and for all that the vast majority of Christians (including conservative evangelicals) do not always use literalistic interpretations of Scripture. Precaution is therefore necessary since the same rule of interpretation is not always, in every instance, justifiable. If we are to arrive at the truth, poetry, prophecy, didactic statement, parable, apocalyptic vision, or gospel narrative demand separate treatment in interpretation.

A second weakness in the dispensational approach is that there seems to be the doctrine that God has two ongoing purposes, one for the church and one for Israel. The church was placed in the world so that through it Christ's message might come to the world (Matt. 28:16-20). By removing the church from the total plan of redemption, dispensationalism has restricted the role of the church in a way not taught previously in the Christian faith.

Third, dispensationalism interprets the millennial kingdom in distinctly Jewish concepts with the land occupied, the throne of David established again, the temple restored and even the sacrifices reinstituted. However, the book of Hebrews makes it clear that the types and shadows of the Old Testament dispensation are forever done away as a means of access to God because of their fulfillment in Christ. Thus dispensationalism removes the church from the redemptive plan of God which was begun in Israel and interprets the purpose of the millennium solely as the literal fulfillment of the Abrahamic and Davidic covenants.

Fourth, there seems to be two ways of salvation taught in the dispensational program, one for the Jews and one for the Gentiles. The emphasis dispensationalists place on the difference between law and grace, between Israel and the church, between the different relations of God to men in different dispensations, when carried to its logical conclusion will lead inevitably to a multiple form of salvation, that men are not saved in the same way in all ages.

Fifth, there is the teaching of a secret coming of Jesus for the church prior to the tribulation which is not supported in Scripture. This teaching of a pretribulation rapture of the church is rooted in the principle of interpretation which separates the church from the total redemptive plan of God. "Our blessed hope" is the second coming of Jesus Christ and not a pretribulation rapture (Titus 2:13). The blessed hope of the believer is not deliverance from the tribulation but union with the Lord at his coming.

These weaknesses, and there may be others, are sufficient to suggest some basic areas of difficulty in the dispensational approach to interpreting biblical eschatology.

Systematic Eschatology

A number of Christian scholars have sought to interpret eschatology by discussing certain events in what appears from Scripture to be the order of occurrence. This approach is what we call "systematic eschatology." Augustus Strong's teaching of eschatology in his book *Systematic Theology* illustrates this method.

The Bible, while not giving minute details, does give a broad outline of the future consummation. There are certain major events taking place in preparation for the completion of the kingdom of God. These events are: death, Christ's second coming, the resurrection, and the last judgment. There will also be an intermediate state as well as a final state, both for the righteous and the unrighteous.

Death. Physical death is the separation of the soul from the body. For the unbeliever physical death is seen as the original penalty of sin, but for the believer in Christ, physical death becomes an entrance into eternal life. Man's soul is immortal and nowhere does Scripture teach that man's soul ceases to exist at death. After studying the scriptural teaching of Jesus' resurrection, A. H. Strong concludes by stating:

> Immortality had been a truth dimly recognized, suspected, longed for before Christ came; but it was he who first brought it out from obscurity and uncertainty into clear daylight and convincing power. Christ's resurrection, moreover, carries with it the resurrection of his people.[15]

The intermediate state is the state of the soul, without a body, between death and resurrection. The intermediate state is for the righteous a state of conscious joy, and for the wicked a state of conscious suffering. There are several passages such as Luke 23:42–43 and Revelation 2:7 which indicate that at death believers enter Paradise. Paradise is the abode of God and the blessed. Paradise is a place which Christ has gone to prepare, perhaps by taking our friends there before us. While the Scriptures teach that the intermediate state will be one of consciousness both for the righteous and the unrighteous, they also represent this state to be one of incompleteness.

Christ's second coming. The second advent will be a literal and visible event (Acts 1:11; 1 Thess. 4:16; Rev. 1:7; John 5:28-29). Neither the apostles nor Christ taught when the end would be. They declared that men should recognize it possibly at hand and so live in an attitude of constant expectation.

The events preceding the second advent will be the preaching of the gospel in all the world until Jews and Gentiles alike become possessed of its blessings, a corresponding development of evil, and the appearance of a personal antichrist. A. H. Strong would hold to a postmillennial position.

The resurrection. At the second coming of Christ there will be a resurrection of the body, and a reunion of the body with the soul. Both the just and the unjust shall have a part in the resurrection. For the just the resurrection will be for life, for the unjust the resurrection will be for condemnation. Those who are living will receive their resurrection bodies without passing through death. The nature of the believer's resurrection body will be patterned after our Lord's resurrection body.

The last judgment. The last judgment will be a time in which the characters of all men will be made known and they will receive their corresponding destinies. God, in the person of Jesus Christ, will be the judge. The final state of the righteous is the fullness and perfection of holy life, in communion with God and with sanctified spirits. Heaven will be the abode of the righteous and will be a place as well as a state of being. The earth, purified by fire, may become the abode of the saints. The final state of the unrighteous is the loss of all good and the misery of an evil conscience banished from the presence of God.

A positive contribution of systematic eschatology is its attempt to put in a systematic format the Bible's teaching of last things. A systematic format of any kind of Bible teaching is of immense help in studying the Bible. A danger of this kind of format is that it can lead to nothing but proof—texting for a certain position or theological viewpoint. Nevertheless, recognizing its strength and weakness, one can learn from systematic eschatology in its attempt to provide an outline of the Bible's teaching of last things.

In these brief descriptions of certain approaches to interpreting eschatology: consistent eschatology, realized eschatology, idealized eschatology, dispensational eschatology, and systematic eschatology, it is evident that no one interpretation was totally right or totally wrong. Each approach had strong and weak points. It is the position of this author that inaugurated eschatology remains the best viewpoint to understand the Bible's teaching of last things. It recognizes the strengths of the other types of eschatology and still holds true to the biblical teaching that God's kingdom has come in the ministry of Jesus Christ and that there is yet to come a series of real events in which history will be consummated and eternity begins.

CHAPTER 3

Biblical Understanding
of Eschatology

If a modern multi-level skyscraper complex is to be constructed to withstand physical stresses, certain basic engineering and architectural principles must be followed. If eschatology is to be an integral part of Christian theology and practical Christian experience then certain biblical principles need to be recognized. There are four main principles in our understanding of biblical eschatology.

Biblical Eschatology Is Concerned with History

The eschatology of the New Testament is grounded in the historical elements of the Old Testament. From earliest times Israel's faith exhibited the profound conviction that God acted purposefully in history, guiding events toward the fulfillment of promise. Basic to Israel's faith was God's action at the time of the Exodus when a new creation was called forth out of the most desperate situations. This coming of God into history resulted in the formation of a new people of God called to announce the future kingdom of God. Thus the kingdom of God has its roots in the concept of a people of God that have been called to live under the rule of God. Israel was confident that she would be granted possession of a land, given material blessings by God, and be victorious over her enemies.

For many Israelites the reign of David seemed to be the fulfillment of promise. But its glories did not last. Israel's hope now began to assume new forms. Basic to this hope was the concept of the day of the Lord of which we hear for the first time in Amos (5:18ff). This concept entailed the belief that a day is coming when God would intervene directly in behalf of his people, judging his foes and theirs, making the promises real. But Amos declared that because of Israel's sin the day of the Lord would not be a day of victory but the day of divine judgment (Amos 5:18ff). Hope for the future was now pushed beyond the day of the Lord to a time when God would act in a new and definitive way to redeem his people from bondage and establish his kingdom. The eschatology of the Old Testament is forward-looking, its principal features are those of hope and promise.

While the notes of hope and promise are present in the New Testament, the prominent theme is one of fulfillment in Jesus Christ. With the ministry of Jesus Christ, biblical eschatology reaches its decisive moment. It is by what Jesus teaches and does, by his loving compassion for others as well as his messages of divine forgiveness, and most important, by his death and resurrection that the meaning of the words, "the kingdom of God is at hand" (Mark 1:15) can be understood.

In the death and resurrection of Jesus Christ is the manifestation of God who enters history and human experience to visit and redeem his people in a unique manner decisive for their salvation. In the person of Jesus Christ, in his deeds, in his words, the kingdom of God and its blessings are present and dynamically active among men. However, there are two factors which prevent the kingdom of God from being fully realized in this earthly historical world: the power of sin is still operative even in the Christian, and the power of death still destroys relationships. Thus the eschatology of the New Testament looks forward to the day when the Messiah will return and death itself is destroyed (1 Cor. 15:26).

The New Testament not only looks backward to the Old Testament and at the death and resurrection of Jesus Christ, but it looks forward both to certain eschatological characteristics of the present age as well as to the events of the endtime. Jesus said that the gospel must be preached in all the world before the end comes (Matt. 24:14; Mark 13:10). This is the one great task assigned to the church. It is the eschatological force of the gospel that provides the motivation for missionary preaching. The period between Jesus' resurrection and his return must be occupied with missionary preaching from Jerusalem to the ends of the earth. This period is indeed a time of grace, granted by God, in order that all persons should have an opportunity to hear the gospel. Our missionary preaching, world-wide, brings us ever closer to the day when our Lord will return.

The eschatology of the New Testament also looks forward to that one final event of the endtime, the return of Jesus Christ. This event cannot be spiritualized away into some continued presence of Jesus. There will be a literal, physical, visible return of Jesus Christ not to deal with sin but to complete our salvation (Heb. 9:28). At present our salvation is incomplete for "we ourselves, who have the first fruits of the Spirit, groan inwardly as we wait for adoption as sons, the redemption of our bodies" (Rom. 8:23). The return of Jesus Christ is the unique endtime event.

Biblical Eschatology Is Inaugurated Eschatology

The type of eschatology that maintains the tension between the present reality of the kingdom of God and its future consummation is "inaugurated eschatology." In the person and work of Jesus of Nazareth, the kingdom of God has come to men in history, bringing to them the blessings of God's kingly rule. That which was promised in the Old Testament has been fulfilled in the mission of Jesus Christ. But there is also a sense in which the kingdom of God is still coming when God will reign and his blessings will be enjoyed by those who have responded to Jesus Christ.

The present reality of the kingdom of God is not some abstract concept of God's universal rule, but rather a dynamic power at work among men. We are reminded that the phrase "kingdom of God" implies God's kingly activity for man's redemption. The kingdom of God is the activity of God manifested in a breaking into history and human experience to visit and redeem his people in a manner decisive for their salvation. It is in Jesus' person and message that God's kingly activity has entered history. One cannot separate Jesus' person from his words; he himself is the message he proclaims. Thus, inaugurated eschatology teaches that in Jesus Christ the endtime has come, the eschatological reality of the kingdom of God is a present reality, and that the world lives in the last days.

But inaugurated eschatology also teaches that there is an endtime. There is an eschatological *now*, but there is also an eschatological future. And the final endtime events are in the future. The kingdom is now, but it awaits its final manifestation. The resurrection of Christ inaugurated the new age which now moves forward to its climax in the return of Jesus Christ. What God did in history in Jesus Christ and what he will do at the end of history by the parousia are two aspects of the same redemptive process of God. The God who has acted in history in the resurrection of Jesus Christ will manifest himself in a mighty appearance at the end of history.

Biblical Eschatology Is Rooted in Jesus Christ

The third principle is that biblical eschatology is rooted in Jesus Christ. The idea of "the God who comes" is one of the central characteristics of the Old Testament teaching about God, and it links together history and eschatology. The New Testament continues this idea but the reference is now to Jesus Christ. The presence and activity of Jesus, in some sense and measure, signalizes the eschatological future. How is this accomplished?

First, with the coming of Jesus the kingdom of God comes which is "now" and "not yet."

> God's Kingdom, his reign, will come at the end of the age in a
> mighty irruption into history inaugurating the perfect order of

the age to come. But God's Kingdom, his reign, *has already come* into history in the person and mission of Jesus.[1]

The truth of the kingdom is to be seen in the teaching of Jesus, the power of the kingdom is seen in Jesus' miracles, and the victory of the kingdom is demonstrated by Jesus' casting out he demons. The kingdom does not evolve, it comes and keeps coming. It is a present reality and yet it is a future event.

Second, Christ's eschatological glory is revealed in his transfiguration. In the transfiguration narratives (Matt. 17:1–13; Mark 9:2–13; Luke 9:28–36) there is a glimpse of the future eschatological glory of Jesus Christ. This temporary exhibition of Jesus' glory was an anticipation of the resurrection and of the parousia, but at the same time it was a revelation of the glory which even then, before his death, belonged to Jesus. In the Gospels Jesus is the lowly one, the rejected one. He will be crucified in weakness. He will be raised from the dead but the world will not receive him. But the day will come when Christ shall appear in glory and power and every eye shall see him (Rev. 1:7). A glimpse of Jesus' future glory was given in the transfiguration.

Third, in the resurrection of Jesus Christ the endtime becomes a reality. The resurrection of Jesus Christ from the dead is an eschatological event. In the resurrection of Jesus the endtimes are present. In this eschatological event the power of sin and death was dissipated. The resurrection of Jesus Christ was, for the first Christians, an eschatological act of God that was as new as the act of creation. It was an act in which Jesus Christ, as the strong Son of God destroyed sin and death and inaugurated the new age. Christ is now King and Lord (Acts 2:32–36) and his return will be the realization of the status he now holds by virtue of his resurrection.

Fourth, the central eschatological event will be the visible personal return of Jesus Christ. That which the transfiguration prefigured, which the kingdom anticipates, and which the resurrection promised will be fulfilled in the parousia of Christ. The parousia of Christ will be the world wide manifestation of his glory (Matt. 24:30; Titus 2:13). The parousia of Jesus Christ is the supreme eschatological event. It will mark the end of the present age and the beginning of the age to come.

Biblical Eschatology Completes God's Redemptive Process

The fourth principle is that biblical eschatology completes God's redemptive process. The story of Israel in the Old Testament is the history of God's activity in saving his chosen people from their enemies, material, and spiritual. The saving acts of God had been experienced at a known place, from a known danger, at a known time, by a known person (Ps. 44:1-3). Abraham is called by God to a new land (Gen. 12:1). Moses is called by God to lead a people out of captivity to a new land as a new people of God. God's saving acts were experienced by Israel in unusual ways, and the Israelites experienced the reality that salvation is only of the Lord.

But the Bible also records the reality of sin and evil. Men are blinded and deceived and finally led away from God by sin and evil powers. Jeremiah perceived the seriousness of sin and evil when he said, "The heart is deceitful above all things, and desperately corrupt; who can understand it?" (Jer. 17:9). Sin breaks the fellowship between men and alienates them from God and earns his wrath (Gen. 3; Jer. 17:5-6; Rom. 3:23; 6:23). Once this becomes clear to man he realizes that there is nothing he can do about his situation. Only God can restore the lost fellowship. Only God can deliver men from the bondage and decay of sin and evil. The remedy can only come from a redeeming God and only in a relationship of forgiveness. The God who acted to redeem his people from bondage in the Old Testament has acted in a new and decisive way to redeem his people from the bondage of sin and death. The New Testament bears witness to God's coming in Jesus to save people from their sins (Matt. 1:21; Luke 1:68-79).

The basic meaning of "salvation" has the sense of deliverance and preservation, of deliverance from enemies or death and preservation in danger. It is a word that can be expressed in three tenses: a past event, "we were saved" (Rom. 8:24); a present experience, "by which you are saved" (1 Cor. 15:2); a future hope, "much more shall we be saved" (Rom. 5:9). Indeed the total scope of salvation is summed up by Paul when he states:

> Therefore, since we are justified by faith, we have peace with God through our Lord Jesus Christ. Through him we have obtained access to this grace in which we stand, and we rejoice in our hope of sharing the glory of God.
>
> (Rom. 5:1-2)

Salvation can be described in many ways using different words. "Redemption" (Rom. 3:24; Col. 1:14), "justified/justification" (Rom. 3:24; 5:1; Gal. 2:16), and "reconciliation" (Rom. 5:10ff; 2 Cor. 5:18-20) are words describing the past event of our salvation. Redemption is a word that comes from the slave market and it pictures a person being set free; justification is a term from the law court and has the sense of a guilty man being acquitted; and reconciliation, a term from the realm of personal relations, means that an estranged person is restored to favor. These three metaphors express the way in which God through Christ delivers sinners from their sin.

The present experience of salvation can be expressed in terms of "life" and "freedom." The newness of life is a life lived in the fellowship with God through Christ, a life liberated from the power of sin (Rom. 6). This new life is energized by the power of the Holy Spirit (Rom. 15:13) which inspires (Gal. 5:22-23) and enables persons to fulfill the Law's demands (Rom. 8:4) while at the same time providing a guarantee of eternal life (Rom 8:11; 2 Cor. 5:5; Eph. 1:14). This new life is a life of freedom from the bondage of sin. Freedom comes only through Christ (Gal. 5:1) and by faith the believer enters into freedom through Christ. The community of believers, the church, not only has the responsibility to proclaim the risen Christ's lordship over the world but also to liberate men for the coming salvation in faith and hope. The eschatological hope promised in the New Testament provides the motivation for and participation in mission.

The future expectation of salvation can be expressed as conforming to the image of Christ (Rom. 8:29). Believers, while experiencing salvation in the past and present, are nevertheless undergoing a process of being changed from one degree of glory to another so that one day they shall be conformed to his image (2 Cor. 3:18). The eschatological character of our salvation can be summed up in the words of John:

> Beloved, we are God's children now; it does not yet appear what we shall be, but we know that when he appears we shall be like him, for we shall see him as he is.
>
> (1 John 3:2)

Thus the consummation of our salvation awaits the endtime eschatological event at which time we will be transformed into the complete image of Jesus Christ.

In summary, our understanding of biblical eschatology contains four elements: first, it is grounded in history and thus has a view of history; second, it adopts the position of inaugurated eschatology which maintains the biblical tension between the present reality of God's kingdom and its future consummation; third, biblical eschatology is centered in the person and work of Jesus Christ; and fourth, biblical eschatology portrays the completion of God's redemptive process for man and creation.

We are now ready to discuss the events of biblical eschatology.

PART II

EVENTS
IN A
BIBLICAL ESCHATOLOGY

§

CHAPTER 4

Death

We now will outline what we can hope for, but in doing so care must be taken against two extremes: undue restraint and a "travelog" eschatology. Undue restraint is characterized by the position that all we can say about life beyond death is that God who was good to us in this life will be good to us after death. This view does not reflect what the New Testament says about the endtime. In many places the New Testament speaks of a second coming, resurrection, heaven and hell, judgment, and a new creation. We cannot bypass these concepts and assume that we have done justice to the biblical teaching.

On the other hand neither can we use the biblical teaching to establish a travelog eschatology. A travelog eschatology is a human construction of future events in daring and vivid colors predicting what is actually going to happen. The proclamation of Jesus was essentially a proclamation that enabled man to reach the endtime, not to calculate the coming of the endtime. With the exception of the book of Revelation, the New Testament shared this restraint with Jesus. Still, some statements need to be made about the endtime. In doing so we will talk only about what God has spoken to us, recognizing the fact that God has spoken in language, symbols, and concepts comprehensible to the human mind. We are to remember statements about eschatological events are by necessity only inadequate approximations of what the endtime is all about.

Ordinarily, death is a universally lamented event in human experience. It is a phenomenon which cannot be accepted as wholly natural, but as a mystery which calls for an explanation. If man was truly "made . . . little less than God" and crowned "with glory and honor," as expressed by the Psalmist (Ps. 8:5), then why should he have a shorter existence than some forms of plant and animal life? And if man was made in the "image of God" (Gen. 1:27) then why must he perish at all? We turn to the Bible to find an answer to these questions and will look first at the Old Testament idea concerning death.

The Old Testament View
A basic affirmation about man in the Old Testament is that he is a creature and as such shares in the feebleness and limitations of all creatures. But alongside of man's creatureliness the Old Testament proclaims an eminent dignity conferred upon him by God. What separates man from the creatures is his status as living beings created in the image of God (Gen. 1:27; Ps. 8). This is why man, although subject to the laws which govern the realm of created things, is yet nearer to God than other creatures.

What man has in common with the animals is flesh, the material manifestation of the body. But what distinguishes man from the animals is the breath of life breathed into him by God, and "man became a living being" (Gen. 2:7). It is man alone that receives the vital breath in his nostrils direct from God, which is proof that God considers him an individual, while animals are created in conformity with the species. Man alone then is a living being, given the breath of life by God.

The most basic observation is that breath is always reckoned the most obvious manifestation of life. This observation conveys that God has transferred from himself into man the life force which God alone can give. Death then is seen as the departure of this life force, the absence of breath. Deprived of life and breath, man is left only with flesh, and as soon as this ceases to be animated, it is in no way distinct from dust. Deprived of the principle of life, the various elements comprising men are "like water spilt on the ground, which cannot be gathered up again" (2 Sam. 14:14). Man reduced to dust is nothing; he no longer exists, and we must not be surprised that several texts speak of death as non-existence; at least that is the conclusion reached by Job and the Psalmist (Job 7:21; Ps. 39:13).

However, another view developed in Israelite thought that seemed to counterbalance this one. Man was seen more as a whole being rather than as a collection of various elements. Man dies, but he does not cease to exist. This existence after death is only a shadow of the existence of the living; but the dead have the same physical characteristics as when they were alive (Gen. 37:35; 42:38; 44:29; 1 Kings 2:6; Ezek. 32:27). Death is seen as the state in which the forces of life are at their lowest intensity, so crushed and drained away as to be virtually absent. This view sees death, not as a brutal and irremediable end of existence as in the former view, but rather as another form of existence in the realm of the dead, Sheol.

Sheol in the Old Testament is pictured as the eternal amoral abode of both the righteous and unrighteous dead. In Sheol there is neither punishment nor reward. The location of Sheol was thought to be a place deep under the earth's surface (Deut. 32:22; Isa. 14:9; 15; Ps. 63:9; 88:6). Sheol is a place of forgetfulness, a land of darkness and dust (Job 10:21–22; 38:17), where there is "no work or thought or knowledge or wisdom" (Eccl. 9:10; cf. also Isa. 38:18). While the existence in Sheol was seen as the negative replica of earthly existence, certain social and national distinctions were maintained (Isa. 14; Ezek. 32), and the dead welcomed new arrivals (Isa. 14:9). Men exist in Sheol but in a form that cannot be called life. They are sunken powerless beings from whom the life forces are gone (Isa. 14:9–10).

But Old Testament faith did not regard death as ultimate separation from God. The Song of Hannah, "The Lord kills and brings to life; he brings down to Sheol and raises up" (1 Sam. 2:6) is an expression of this faith. Other expressions of this faith are expressed by Job, "I shall see God" (Job 19:26) and by the Psalmist (Ps. 73:21–28). In reference to Job's affirmation "I shall see God," means that to see God, at least in this text, is to share in his life, and, since God does not die, he who is in communion with God finds death powerless to destroy life. An experience similar to Job's is that of the Psalmist (Ps. 16) who expresses the conviction that Sheol will have no power over him, since he is destined to life and this life is communion with the living God. In Psalm 73 the author affirms that God will stay with him even when his body crumbles to dust (Ps. 73:26). Thus, some believers in the Old Testament expressed the faith that even death could not separate them from God.

In spite of this positive expression of faith there seems to be no clear doctrine of life after death for the individual in the early thought of the Old Testament. The taking up of Enoch and Elijah to fellowship with God (Gen. 5:24; 2 Kings 2:11) does not express resurrection hope, but it could stimulate men into thinking that God's people will have a privileged position in living with him. The raising of a child by Elijah and by Elisha (1 Kings 17:17–23; 2 Kings 4:32–36) may have created an atmosphere congenial to the idea of resurrection. However, the hope of resurrection, only glimpsed earlier, becomes clear in two Old Testament passages. In Isaiah resurrection is promised only to the righteous (Isa. 26:16–19) while the wicked are expressly excluded (Isa. 26:10–14). This passage in Isaiah has been referred to as the earliest direct reference to the resurrection.[1] The second passage is in Daniel 12:2, "And many of those who sleep in the dust of the earth shall awake, some to everlasting life, and some to shame and everlasting contempt." "The reference here is not to the general resurrection but rather to the fact that salvation will be not only for those who were alive but also for some who lost their lives during the persecution."[2] In these two passages we observe that until the day of resurrection, the shades of all who have died remain in Sheol. Behind both passages lies the belief that the righteous man's communion with God cannot be destroyed by death.

The relationship between sin and death is undeveloped in the Old Testament. Only in the latest Old Testament texts does the concept emerge that sin always produces a state of weakness which is a forerunner of death. Sin is seen as the breaking of a relationship between man and God and when this happens man is delivered to himself or to evil forces. In the Genesis story (Gen. 3) sin is seen as the refusal to choose God and this results in the breaking of the relationship between God and man. Thus it seems that the manifold, profound troubles in human life have their root in the one trouble of man's relationship to God. Expressed more concisely, Genesis, Chapter 3, asserts that all sorrow comes from sin. When we get to the New Testament, the direct link between sin and death is made clear (Rom. 6:23).

The New Testament View

The view of death in New Testament times was little different from that in the Old Testament. People were still slaves to the fear of death. We catch a glimpse into the mourning when death visited the home in several passages in the New Testament. We see this in the weeping over the death of Lazarus (John 11:19ff) and the daughter of Jairus (Mark 5:38). There was little in the religion of the people to remove this fear and dread of death.

But in Jesus' view of death and the teachings of the New Testament, death loses its fearsome aspect. Death is not always a welcomed event, but when it does appear, it has lost its power to enslave men with fear. There is no philosophy of death in the New Testament. What the New Testament speaks of is the promise of continuous communion for the believer with God. There are no biblical grounds for saying that "death means the end"; there are biblical grounds for saying that death ushers a person into a new sphere of life.

Nevertheless, when we speak of death, we speak of the cessation of life in the form we know it. "It is the disembodiment of man in his historical and earthly existence, the severance of the self from its origin of expression."[3] The Greek word *thanatos,* translated death, means a separation (whether natural or violent) of the soul from the body by which the life on earth is ended. Soul would refer to the entire person whereas spirit would refer to that which gives life to the body, the spiritual side of man. Several Scripture passages illustrate the validity of this definition. James wrote, ". . . the body apart from the spirit is dead" (James 2:26). Jesus on the cross said, " 'Father into thy hands I commit my spirit!' And having said this he breathed his last" (Luke 23:46). The story of the rich fool (Luke 12:16–20) is another example. When his spirit was called from his body, his body ceased to be and his wealth was of no use to him. The thrust of these passages simply points up the fact that at death there is a separation of the spirit from the body which brings to an end life and activity on this material plane.

Jesus referred to death as sleep. At the raising of Jairus' daughter, he said regarding her, ". . . the girl is not dead but sleeping" (Matt. 9:24; cf. also Mark 5:39; Luke 8:52). When Lazarus died, Jesus said to his disciples, "Our friend Lazarus has fallen asleep, but I go to awake him out of sleep" (John 11:11). The disciples thought that Jesus meant Lazarus was in a coma or had some serious illness. Jesus corrected the disciples' misunderstanding by stating that "Lazarus is dead" (John 11:14). Jesus was presenting to his people a view of death as something which was not to be feared as a great enemy. This view of death as sleep portrays the cessation of strife and all other activities of life. In using the metaphor of sleep to describe death, Jesus was saying that as a sleeper does not cease to exist while his body sleeps, so a dead person continues to exist despite the absence of bodily functions. The spirits of the dead, "those who sleep" exist in the intermediate state waiting for the resurrection of the body. The fear of death has not disappeared, but for the believer death has lost its horror, its "sting" (1 Cor. 15:54-57).

> The Christian is not exempt from the experience of dying but he is exempt from its sting. Having been united with the crucified and risen Lord he is passed beyond all the threat and terror of death.[4]

Paul used Jesus' terminology in referring to death as sleep. Writing to the church in Thessalonica, Paul declared that "those who are asleep" (1 Thess. 4:13) will experience all the glory of the Lord's return. In Acts 7:60 the death of Stephen is described in the words, "he fell asleep."

Jesus and Paul, in using the metaphor of sleep to describe death are attempting to remove the fear of the unknown for Christians. However, death involves the whole person, body and spirit. Our bodies, constituted as they are, are subject to physical decay and death. Our spirits survive the event of physical death and it is with this spiritual nature of a person that Paul now addresses himself. The Bible faces death as it faces all reality. But the emphasis of the Bible is that life and death are treated as that from which a person is saved.

Paul also believed that death was the result of sin, "the wages of sin is death" (Rom. 6:23). The word *opsonion*, translated wages, denotes that which is due, a compensation for services rendered. This expression gives us the thought that sin not only results in death, but that it deserves to result in death. Physical death is a symbol of a deeper spiritual truth. Man, because he is sinful man, lives only within the sphere of death, and he must regard himself as condemned to death. This body and death cannot be separated. Thus death can be seen as the end of a sinful alienation of man from God. Death as the end of this life means the end of the possibility of sinning, the end of our shortcomings, and the end of our continuous estrangement from God.

Another relationship between sin and death can be seen in Paul's view that men are slaves of sin unto death (Rom. 6:16, 20). Jesus also taught that men can be enslaved by sin (John 8:34). The impact of these verses is that man is enslaved to sin and he cannot avoid death. Physically he is condemned to death and spiritually he is already dead. He is ruled by death, by that death which can be spoken of as "the last enemy" (1 Cor. 15:26). For Paul the entire human race is involved in sin (Rom. 3:23) and death has its sway over all men (Rom. 5:12–14).

We all die, and each one of us dies alone; death proves to the individual that he is finite.

Deliverance from death is a major truth of the gospel. We read in the Old Testament that the defeat of death is seen as the great manifestation of God's power of life, glory, and mercy. The prophet looked forward to the time when God "will swallow up death for ever" and there will be no more tears and heartache (Isa. 25:8). The New Testament bears witness to the fact that in Jesus Christ death was abolished and life and immortality were achieved for all believers (2 Tim. 1:10). Paul understood Jesus' death as solving the problem of sin (Rom. 6:10; 2 Cor. 5:21). The author of Hebrews states that:

> Since therefore the children share in flesh and blood, he himself likewise partook of the same nature, that through death he might destroy him who has the power of death, that is, the devil, and deliver all those who through fear of death were subject to lifelong bondage.
>
> (Heb. 2:14-15)

The biblical texts make it clear that the death of Jesus has been instrumental in delivering men from the sphere of death.

> Death is, in fact, what some modern people call "ambivalent." It is Satan's great weapon and also God's great weapon: it is holy and unholy; our supreme disgrace and our only hope; the thing Christ came to conquer and the means by which He conquered.[5]

In Jesus' death and resurrection sin and death were conquered (Rom. 6:9). The promise is given that death itself will ultimately be destroyed (1 Cor. 15:26; Rev. 21:4).

> The important teaching of the New Testament is not that death is an evil, or that man cannot overcome it, but that death has been decisively defeated in the atoning death of the Saviour, who "abolished death, and brought life and incorruption to light through the gospel" (2 Tim. 1:10).[6]

While the body is subject to death, the spirit is not (Rom. 8:10) and in God's own time the body is to be transformed so that it can never be subject to death again. Paul knew that God gave a body to his spirit in this life. He also knew that God would give a new body to his spirit for the next life. This resurrection body would be given at the resurrection of the dead (1 Cor. 15). Paul saw then that to depart from this life was for the spirit to lay aside the body and enter a conscious existence until the resurrection body is given. Although Paul did not desire this intermediate state, nevertheless he believed that to be absent from the body is to be at home with the Lord (Phil. 1:23).

In the next chapter we turn to the biblical teaching of the intermediate state, the state of the spirit between death and resurrection.

CHAPTER 5

The Intermediate State

In the preceding pages we learned that the reality of death is one event all persons encounter. We also learned that for the believer, death has lost its terror because of what God has done for us in Jesus Christ. It has also been noted that a person's spirit survives physical death. Now if this is true, and the Bible indicates that it is true, then at death, where do these spirits go?

What is central in the Bible about the future of man is the teaching of the return of Christ and the events that accompany that return: the resurrection, the last judgment, and the creation of the new earth. But before we can consider these events we must give some attention to what is commonly called "the intermediate state."

The intermediate state can be defined as that state of spiritual existence which the individual experiences in the interim between his death and his resurrection. The intermediate state is a state of another time-consciousness in which believers are nearer Christ. This intermediate state, however, is not the hope of the Christian but simply a state in which the spirit of the person exists awaiting the resurrection of the body.

There are students of the Bible who believe that there is no biblical basis for a teaching of an intermediate state. Some would argue that when a person dies, the "natural body" is immediately replaced by a "spiritual body." The basis for this belief is a reluctance to accept the idea of a spirit's having life apart from the body. Those who hold this view cite 2 Corinthians 5:1-4 and understand the spiritual body to be the "building from God, a house not made with hands" (2 Cor. 5:1). They believe that this spiritual body will be exchanged for the eternal body at the time of resurrection.

Other students of the Bible who reject the idea of an intermediate state do so on the basis that there is only one reality after death for believers, and that is the resurrection of the body. They reject the idea that "something" of man persists after death upon which God will fashion a new creation. They would argue that according to Scripture, a person dies totally with body and spirit. To speak of continuity between present life and the life of the resurrection body is misleading. God does not need to create a resurrection body out of something, i.e., our spirits, or our personality. He can create out of nothing a new life. Therefore, to talk of an intermediate state is to speak of something foreign to the Bible.

Other Bible students who reject the doctrine of the intermediate state do so on the grounds that this teaching is not biblical. They state that the doctrine of the intermediate state does not do justice to the seriousness of death, since the soul passes through death untouched. They further argue that by teaching that a spirit without a body can be blessed and happy, the significance of the resurrection body is denied. Furthermore, it is stated that the doctrine of the intermediate state is individualistic. It involves a personal kind of blessedness rather than fellowship with others. Therefore, the teaching of the intermediate state must be rejected because it destroys what belongs together: the spirit and body, the individual and community, and blessedness and final glory.

One other viewpoint must be noted. Some who reject the doctrine of the intermediate state do so on the grounds that the Bible does not speak of a conscious state of a person's spirit after death. The interval between death and resurrection is like the experience of sleep. A person goes to sleep and after a few hours awakens without consciousness of a time lapse and without consciousness of what has happened to him during sleep. So, a believer who dies will sleep until the Lord comes and knocks on his grave and calls him to rise to new life. Those who hold this view would state that those who die are in a sense "out of time" as we know it and therefore one cannot project our understanding of time into their interim after death with a doctrine of an intermediate state.

From the preceding paragraphs one realizes that the doctrine of the intermediate state is not accepted by all Bible students. It is not our purpose to interact with these various views but to simply state them to illustrate the fact that not all Christians accept the doctrine of the intermediate state. For those who would like to see the critique of these views I would refer them to the following books listed in the bibliography: *The Return of Christ* by G. C. Berkouwer, *The Bible and the Future,* by Anthony H. Hoekema, and *The Last Things* by George E. Ladd.

It is true that there are not many references in the New Testament concerning the intermediate state, perhaps due to the fact that this is only a temporary condition. Rather, the New Testament focuses on the return of Christ and the new age that is to follow. There are, however, several references that do speak of the intermediate state as a state of conscious existence for both the unrighteous and the righteous. They do not solve all the problems nor give all the answers, but they do shed some light on the state of the individual existence between death and resurrection. We will consider first the passages relating to the unrighteous and then those relating to the righteous.

The State of the Unrighteous

There are only a few New Testament passages concerning the intermediate state of the unrighteous. The few which do relate to the topic lead to several conclusions.

First, there is the concept that the unrighteous are separated from God. This concept is illustrated in the story of Lazarus and the rich man (Luke 16:19–31). At death Lazarus was carried to the bosom of Abraham, and Lazarus was separated from the rich man by an impassable gulf. The blessings of Lazarus in the presence of God were denied the rich man in this separation. Second, this story also indicates that the rich man, as well as Lazarus, is alive and conscious. In the story the rich man was conscious of his surroundings and his condition. Third, the rich man was conscious of his suffering. He now experiences such misery that he begs for help, even if it is only a single drop of water for his thirsty tongue. In 2 Peter 2:9 there is an indication that God keeps the unrighteous under punishment until the day of judgment. This verse seems to refer to the wretched existence of the wicked between their death and the final judgment.

What can be said of the place where the unrighteous undergo this punishment? In Luke 16:23 the rich man is said to be in Hades. Hades is to be understood as "the abode of the departed." It is the Greek counterpart to the Old Testament Sheol. Later on it became the name of the realm of the dead itself. The word Hades is used ten times in the New Testament in the following ways:

1. As a general reference to the grave: Acts 2:27, 31; Rev. 1:18; 6:8.
2. As a reference to the place of the departed wicked: Luke 16:23; Rev. 20:14.
3. As a general reference to death or extinction: Matt. 11:23; Luke 10:15; Matt. 16:18; Rev. 20:13.

From the way Hades is used by the writers of the New Testament, we need to be careful about drawing hard and fast conclusions. Nevertheless I believe that the New Testament indicates that unbelievers go to the realm of the dead (Hades) when they die, where, already plunged into affliction, they are to await the final judgment (Rev. 20:13, 14).

For the unbeliever the intermediate state means an existence far from God. This state is characterized as one of waiting in distress for God's final judgment of rejection. Walter Kunneth describes this state of the unrighteous as

an existence of dire tension, of torturing unrest in the
knowledge of having failed to attain life's goal—an existence in
which our utter and complete dependence on the Risen one is
made unsparingly plain. This state of waiting in "hell" "between" death and resurrection . . . implies a clarification of
man's in itself hopeless situation in the light of the resurrection
of Jesus.[1]

The State of the Righteous

It has been observed earlier that at death bodily activity
ceases and the spirit enters into a conscious state of existence.
The nature of this state for the righteous will now be looked at.

First, the spirits of the righteous are with God. In Philippians 1:23 Paul spoke of departing to be with Christ. The di-
lemma Paul faced was that while living in this world he could
be of further service to Christ. On the other hand, death is
sheer gain, because as Paul believed, beyond death is the im-
mediate presence of Christ. The same idea is expressed in 2
Corinthians 5:8 where Paul spoke of being away from the body
and at home with the Lord. Paul understood that at death he
would give up the body and be with the Lord. In Luke 23:43
Jesus told the penitent thief that he will be with him in paradise. In Luke 16:22 the phrase "Abraham's bosom" is a figura-
tive expression referring to the presence of God. The emphasis
of these texts indicates that the righteous enter immediately
at death into the presence of God.

Second, the spirits of the righteous are in paradise. The word
"paradise" is of Persian origin and has the meaning of garden
or park, a place of beauty and enjoyment. In the Greek Old
Testament "paradise" is used to represent the garden of Eden
in Genesis 2:8. Paradise is used three times in the New Testament. In Luke 23:43 Jesus used this word to assure the thief
that he would be with him. The thief was to enter the "abode of
the righteous," with Jesus. In 2 Corinthians 12:4 Paul describes an experience in which he was "caught up into paradise." Whatever Paul experienced, he was not allowed to make
known to men. God has not permitted the veil which conceals
the mysteries and glories of heaven to be raised. In Revelation

2:7 the one who overcomes is assured that he will eat of the tree of life "which is in the paradise of God." Paradise is used in reference to bliss in the presence of God himself. These references appear to indicate that paradise is the place where God dwells. It is indicated also that the righteous at death go immediately to be in the presence of God in paradise.

Third, the spirits of the righteous are alive and conscious. In Luke 16:22-23 Jesus represented Lazarus as alive and conscious in "Abraham's bosom." Jesus' statement in Matthew 22:32 that God is the God of the living implies that although the patriarchs had died physically long ago they are still in some sense alive. Paul believed that if he was to die then his death would be gain for him since he would be in the presence of the Lord. This would be better only if Paul could consciously experience the presence of the Lord beyond death. Fourth, the spirits of the righteous are at rest. In Revelation 14:13 we read, " 'Blessed are the dead who die in the Lord henceforth.' 'Blessed indeed,' says the Spirit, 'that they may rest from their labors, for their deeds follow them!' " The idea expressed here is that the righteous are refreshed after their labors even to the point of exhaustion. Those who die in the Lord are said to be in a blessed state refreshed from their labors.

While the state of the righteous is one of conscious existence in the presence of God, a state of blessedness, rest, and joy, nevertheless it is an incomplete state. As in this life, so in death, there is the tension between the "already" and the "not yet." In the intermediate state the blessedness is indeed there, but the crown has not yet been attained. The endowment of the crown will be postponed until later, until the return of the Lord. The intermediate state for the righteous is not yet the final goal, not yet that which has been promised.

> It is a partial anticipation of the consummation in the form of communion with Christ—it is a preconsummation—but not yet the resurrection of the body, not yet the glorification which is bound up with the appearing of Jesus.[2]

"For we know that if the earthly tent we live in is destroyed, we have a building from God, a house not made with hands, eternal in the heavens" (2 Cor. 5:1).

A Look at the Concept of Purgatory

The concept of purgatory presupposes an intermediate state between death and resurrection. The traditional doctrine of purgatory was enunciated by the Roman Catholic Church by action of the Second Council of Lyons, Benedict XII's *Benedictus Deus*, and the Council of Florence in A.D. 1439.[3] Purgatory is defined as "the place and state in which souls are purged after death because of their sins, before they go to heaven."[4]

The origin of this concept goes back to the intertestamental period. In the second book of Maccabees we read:

> For if he were not expecting that those who had fallen would rise again, it would have been superfluous and foolish to pray for the dead. But if he was looking to the splendid reward that is laid up for those who fall asleep in godliness, it was a holy and pious thought. Therefore, he made atonement for the dead, that they might be delivered from their sin.
>
> (2 Macc. 12:44–45)

In this passage the religious practice of praying for the dead is first mentioned and sanctioned. Trying to find a scriptural basis for the concept of purgatory presents some difficulty. One Roman Catholic scholar, Joseph Pohle, is convinced that Matthew 12:32 provides New Testament support for the doctrine of purgatory. He believes that the "world to come" plainly means life after death. He then states, "Hence, according to our Saviour's own testimony, there must be some sins that are forgiven after death."[5] The editors of the *Catholic Biblical Encyclopedia* state that Matthew 12:32 implies the existence of purgatory and that our Lord speaks of the possibility of the guilt of sin being forgiven in the next world.[6] However, many biblical commentators do not find any support in this verse for the doctrine of purgatory.

Modern emphasis on the doctrine of purgatory by Roman

Catholic scholars sees purgatory as a state of cleansing suffering when purification and growth take place. As the relationship between Christ and the church also includes the dead in Christ, then prayer for them is meaningful if it actualizes the church's essence. Purgatory then is:

> ... the state in which those who have died in the Lord wait for the individual and universal consummation. Prayer for the dead in purgatory would thus in another form be prayer for the second coming of the Lord (Rev. 22:17). As such it would possess an individual meaning in the highest degree.[7]

As we have seen earlier death is not a transitional state in which life continues on similar to life on earth. Rather death is to be seen as a rupture and a dimensional borderline beyond which there is something radically different than what we have experienced here on earth. When God chose the stage of history for the salvation of man, he sealed forever the decisiveness of this present life and the eternal consequences of the decisions made here about Christ. Any thinking of extending our influence on the destiny of those beyond death would do away with the radical nature of death as well as affecting the whole attitude of life here on earth.

As it was noted earlier, the doctrine of purgatory presupposes an intermediate state. Nevertheless, the vast majority of Protestants reject the doctrine of purgatory. They do not find any scriptural basis for this unique doctrine. There are, in fact, a number of passages which are at variance with the doctrine of purgatory (Luke 16:26; Matt. 25:1-13; Rom. 3:28; Gal. 2:21; Heb. 9:27-28; Rev. 22:11). The majority of Protestants thus reject any doctrine of purgatory since they believe that it is without valid biblical justification. They stand firm on the conviction that Jesus did not teach a doctrine of purgatory. The apostle Paul sums up the position of those who reject the doctrine of purgatory when he states: "For by grace you have been saved through faith; and this is not your own doing, it is the gift of God—not because of works, lest any man should boast" (Eph. 2:8-9).

CHAPTER 6

The Second Coming
of Jesus

The term "second coming" is not found in the New Testament, nevertheless its truth occupies a prominent place in the New Testament teaching about Christ. Following the ascension of Jesus, his disciples made much of the promise of his return. The promise of Jesus' return is reflected in their preaching and in their writings as apostles. The emphasis of the New Testament is on a personal, visible, and triumphant return of Jesus Christ to the earth to consummate God's purpose in history and to usher in the eternal order.

What does the New Testament say about the return of Jesus Christ? A word often used in the New Testament for the Lord's return is "*erchomi*" which has the meaning "I come." This word is used in Matthew 24 and 25 by Jesus when he spoke of the coming of worldly masters after a journey. Jesus used these illustrations to speak of his own coming.

There are three other words used in the New Testament which have a bearing on the doctrine of the second coming. One is "*epiphaneia*" which means appearing or appearance. The word is used in 2 Timothy 1:10 to refer to the coming of Christ. In five other passages it is used to refer to the second coming of Christ (1 Tim. 6:14; 2 Tim. 4:1, 8; 2 Thess. 2:8; Titus 2:13). Another word is *"apokalupsis"* which means a revelation or disclosure. It is used in 1 Peter 4:13 as the revelation of the glory of God belonging to the last days. It is also used with reference to the second coming (1 Peter 1:7, 13; 1 Cor. 1:7; 2 Thess. 1:7). A third word is *"parousia"* which means presence, or coming, "advent as the first stage in presence." It was used when a person made a visit to someone (Matt. 24:3, 27, 37, 39). Paul used it to refer to the resurrection at the Lord's coming (1 Cor. 15:23). He used it four times in 1 Thessalonians to speak of the second coming of Christ (2:19; 3:13; 4:15; 5:23). This word is used in other places and each time it has reference to the second coming (2 Thess. 2:1; 2 Peter 1:16; 3:4, 12; 1 John 2:28). These words have but one basic idea and that is that the coming, the appearing, the revealing, and the presence of Christ all point to that one event, the second coming of Christ which is part of the Christian hope.

However, some biblical scholars deny that Jesus ever spoke of returning literally and bodily to the earth. Harold Guy believes that Jesus spoke of judgment and resurrection in the same manner as many of his contemporaries and that never did Jesus say that he himself will return to earth in connection with these events.

> It seems plain that he meant some great event which his contemporaries would witness and experience, but did not mean to be understood as implying a physical "return" or a literal coming to earth of himself.[1]

John A. T. Robinson does not believe in a literal return of Christ. The doctrine of the second coming of Christ simply clarifies what must happen and what is happening whenever Christ comes in love and power. He writes, "The Second Coming has happened in the return of Christ in the Spirit; the Resurrection of the Body has occurred in the putting on of the new man in the Body of Christ."[2] Thus, the viewpoint of some biblical scholars can be summed up in the words of Guy: "We may consider the belief in the future 'coming' of Jesus, whether conceived to be in the first century or after a lapse of centuries, to be a mistaken one."[3]

On the other hand are those scholars who believe that a literal bodily return of Christ is an indispensable part of New Testament doctrine. George Ladd believes that,

> The second coming of Jesus Christ is an absolutely indispensable doctrine in the Biblical teaching of redemption. Apart from His glorious return, God's work will forever be incomplete. At the center of redemption past is Christ on the cross; at the center of redemption future is Christ returning in glory.[4]

G. C. Berkouwer, in his book, *The Return of Christ,* states:

> As a "second coming," then, the parousia is not a mere repetition of His original coming, but the unchallenged revelation and irreversible fulfillment of the meaning and force of reconciliation.[5]

Those who believe in a personal visible return of Jesus Christ would agree with Emil Brunner:

> Faith in Jesus Christ without the expectation of His Parousia is a voucher that is never redeemed, a promise that is not seriously meant. A Christian faith without expectation of the Parousia is like a ladder which leads nowhere but ends in the void.[6]

One theme which remains constant in the New Testament is the certainty of Jesus' return. Jesus spoke of his coming as a matter of certainty (Luke 17:22-37) and he warned his disciples to be watchful (Luke 12:39-40). Those who are not ready will suffer irrevocable loss. The preaching and writings of the apostles also emphasize the certainty of the Lord's return (Acts 3:20; 1 Thess. 4:13-18; Col. 3:1-4). In Acts 1:11 the promise is given that Jesus will return in a manner similar to his going into heaven. The ascension of Jesus Christ anticipates the triumph of his return when he shall bring the kingdom of God to victory.

The certainty of the Lord's return is reflected in Hebrews 9:28. In this passage the author makes the statement that Christ will return a "second" time. This passage settles it for

certain that the New Testament teaches a literal return of
Jesus Christ. His coming will be clear to all, sudden and universally visible so that there will be no room or time for all
kinds of exact prophecies or descriptions of it.

We now turn to discuss several aspects of Jesus' second coming: the time of his coming, the signs of his coming, the rapture, and the antichrist.

The Time of His Coming

There is no part of the doctrine of Jesus' second coming that
has created more interest than the question of the time of his
coming. This is true in spite of the fact that the New Testament reveals little, if anything, about the specific time of the
Lord's return.

Jesus denied the possibility of calculating the date of his
return. In Mark 13:32 we read, "But of that day or that hour
no one knows, not even the angels in heaven, nor the Son, but
only the Father." In this passage Jesus tells the disciples that
the knowledge of the time of his return is hidden from the universe and belongs only to the Father. Jesus makes the same
point in Matthew 24:36. For all the certainty of its coming, the
time of Jesus' return is known only to the Father.

Jesus again emphasizes this idea in Acts 1:7 when the disciples asked if Jesus were going to restore the kingdom to
Israel. Jesus told the disciples that it was not for them to know
when God would consummate his purpose. The disciples were
to be looking for the power to enable them to bear witness to
Christ, not knowledge about God's purposes. The knowledge
of Jesus' return was reserved to the Father alone.

The fact that the time of the Lord's return remains unknown
is stressed in the New Testament. This unknown aspect is not
introduced in a context of secrecy, but in order to extend an
urgent call to watchfulness. "Watch therefore, for you know
neither the day nor the hour" (Matt. 25:13; cf. Mark 13:32ff).
This watchfulness is emphasized in the New Testament because man does not know the day and hour of Jesus' return.

The Signs of His Coming

If we cannot know the definite time of the Lord's return, what can we know about the time of his return? Are there any signs that point toward the return of Jesus? The word *"semeion"* translated sign has the sense of a distinguishing mark, an indication, a token, or an event that is contrary to the usual course of nature. Jesus' teachings were not designed to be a textbook on the chronology of prophecy. It was only in answer to specific questions that Jesus sketched the course of the age and its consummation. It is possible that unnecessary preoccupation with the signs of the times may be an attempt to define and locate the time of the parousia in some sense, even if not attempting to fix the date exactly.

In response to the question of the disciples about the time of his return, Jesus set forth some things concerning the course of this age. This teaching appears in Mark 13, in Matthew 24 and 25, and in Luke 21:5-36. The teachings in these passages are perhaps some of the most difficult in the New Testament. Jesus' teaching was not given to satisfy a curiosity about the future but to emphasize the fact that he will return to earth to bring God's purpose to reality, to warn against being misled by false prophets, to encourage readiness for his return, and to remind his followers of their world mission.

The Synoptic parallels (Matt. 24 and 25; Mark 13; Luke 21:5-36) agree that Jesus spoke about the destruction of Jerusalem and his second coming. Matthew, while following Mark's account, heightens Mark's concern for the return of Christ. Luke, on the other hand, places a greater emphasis on the destruction of Jerusalem. Jesus' discourse on the destruction of Jerusalem appears in Matthew 24:15-28; Mark 13:1-13; and Luke 21:5-24. Jesus' sayings on the second coming appear in Matthew 24:29-44; Mark 13:24-37; and Luke 21:25-36. In two passages it is difficult to discern whether Jesus is talking about the destruction of Jerusalem or the second coming (Matt. 24:3-14; Mark 13:14-23). In response to the disciples' question (Matt. 24:3; Mark 13:4; Luke 21:7) Jesus began his discourse speaking about the destruction of Jerusalem and concluded by speaking of his second coming. While some parts of his discourse may refer to one event or the other, it is clear that at the end of his discourse Jesus is speaking about the second coming of the Son of man.

In the discussion concerning the signs of Jesus' return we will use the account in Mark's Gospel (Mark 13). In this passage Jesus speaks about the destruction of Jerusalem, which occurred in A.D. 70, as a symbol of his own coming in judgment upon the world. He told them that Jerusalem was to be destroyed. He definitely told them that he himself would return in judgment upon the world. But Jesus separated these two events. These two events are related only in the sense that one preceded the other. The destruction of Jerusalem would precede the destruction of the world and one was used to illustrate that destruction and judgment.

In Mark 13:5 Jesus warned his disciples against being led astray by false reports and prophets. Preoccupation with the endtime speculations leaves one vulnerable to false prophets or false christs which usually leads to the neglect of preaching the gospel to all nations. There would be times, such as the destruction of Jerusalem, when people would be disturbed in their thinking, but they were not to be misled. Jesus' words (Mark 13:5) emphasize the true purpose of biblical prophecy which is practical and not speculative. His teaching is given not to enable us to forecast the future but to interpret the present, not to satisfy curiosity but to deliver from perplexity and to encourage watchfulness. Jesus reminds the disciples that as history unfolds there will always be wars and rumors of wars (Mark 13:7; Matt. 24:6). Imposters in the religious sphere, commotions in political and international relations, and disasters in the physical world are part of this age in which we live. Jesus is very clear that these things do not mark the end of the age, they are not to be taken as signs of the end. Mark uses the word *odinon* which means "birthpangs." Mark records Jesus as saying that these things are the beginning of the sufferings that the disciples must endure.

Jesus then warns his followers that they will suffer persecution at the hands of both religious and political leaders.

Nevertheless the gospel must be preached to all nations (Mark 13:10). The word used by Mark for nations comes from *ethnos* which means people, heathen, pagans, or Gentiles. The gospel is destined to be preached to all peoples before the end should come. When the gospel is preached to all peoples then and only then will the end come. However, the church cannot calculate the date of the end by whether or not the gospel has been preached to all peoples. While the thrust of this passage implies that the gospel must be preached to the whole world, there is an indication that the gospel will be preached until the end.

During the time when the church is proclaiming the gospel there will be many trials. Betrayal, hostility, and persecution will sap the loyalty and courage of the disciples (Mark 13:12). To those who endure to the end will go the crown of salvation. This endurance may not mean to the end of the age but rather to the end of one's own life. This endurance lies in the willingness of the believer to bear witness to Jesus Christ right up to his death.

In Mark 13:14ff Jesus refers specifically to the destruction that was to come upon Jerusalem. The city was to be destroyed and the Temple defiled. No doubt Jesus' words reminded the disciples of the time when the Temple was defiled by Antiochus Epiphanes, the Syrian ruler who in 168 B.C. sacrificed a hog on the altar and set up in the Temple an altar to Greek gods. This incident became symbolic of the most arrogant and atrocious affront conceivable to the Jews. In using this symbol Jesus predicted a disaster for his nation. In A.D. 70 the Roman general Titus forced his way into the city destroying it and the Temple. However, it is to be noted that the meaning of Jesus' words cannot be exhausted by referring only to this event. We believe that Jesus was referring, in a secondary sense for the benefit of the church, to the appearing of the antichrist. Perhaps this is the intent of Jesus' words, "let the reader understand" (Mark 13:14).

From this point Jesus goes on to speak of the return in glory of the Son of man (Mark 13:24ff). The tribulation mentioned probably refers to sufferings, persecutions, and temptations endured by Christians for the sake of Christ. Following the tribulation cosmic upheavals prepare the way for the return of Jesus Christ. The universe will veil its light at the appearance of the glory and salvation of the Son of man. The coming of the Son of man on the clouds is his return to earth in power and glory. That he will appear on or with the clouds of heaven emphasizes his being seen. This is also the intent of the promise made to the disciples at Jesus' ascension (Acts 1:11) that his return will be visible for all to see.

Jesus now exhorts the disciples to be watchful (Mark 13:28-37). The parable of the fig tree reminds the disciples to be alert that they may with spiritual insight discern the unfolding of God's purposes in the events of history. Many of Jesus' followers witnessed the destruction of Jerusalem. What now became a reality to them was the certainty of Christ's visible return. But the time of his return is not known, it being locked away in the mind of God (Mark 13:32). The necessity for watchfulness and prayerfulness is again emphasized by Jesus (Mark 13:33ff). The disciples are to live always anticipating difficulty and persecutions but at the same time in confident and expectant hope of the return of Jesus Christ in the consummation of God's purpose.

From this discussion of the signs relating to the second coming of Jesus, it is evident that they are related to the present and to faith. They are not a neutral list of events that can be used to calculate the future. They point to the future, but at the same time they stimulate the direction of every activity that leads to the triumphant and dynamic coming of God's kingdom. The signs point to events already happening which are closely related to the approaching redemption: "When these things begin to take place, look up and raise your heads, because your redemption is drawing near" (Luke 21:28). The point is simply this, that Jesus' return is imminent, the time known only to God. Therefore the disciples must be alert, facing the future without fear, not being led astray (Mark 13:5) but enduring in patience (Mark 13:13). Supported by the Holy

Spirit (Mark 13:11) the disciples will have power and wisdom and soundness of speech that none will be able to destroy (Luke 21:15).

The signs given by Jesus were not given in order that we may calculate his arrival. Rather they are intended to be a summons to watchfulness for the coming of the Lord, a perseverance in the faith, and missionary service in the Lord.

> A hope that is directed entirely to the future paralyses action in the present. It calculates dates but it forgets that Jesus will return when God decides, and not when we try to attract him, to bring him back to earth by our actions or our knowledge.[7]

No matter how carefully history is interpreted and signs calculated, the coming of the end will be a surprise, it will be absolutely unexpected. Perhaps this is what Jesus meant when he said, "Therefore you also must be ready; for the Son of man is coming at an hour you do not expect" (Matt. 24:44; cf. Mark 13:37).

The Rapture

The only place in the New Testament where the rapture is specifically mentioned is in Paul's letter to the Thessalonians. Paul seeks to comfort believers whose loved ones have recently died, with the assurance that at the return of Christ these will be given first consideration: "The dead in Christ will rise first; then we who are alive, who are left, shall be caught up together with them in the clouds to meet the Lord in the air" (1 Thess. 4:16–17). The word *harpazo* means to snatch, seize, i.e., take suddenly and vehemently. In 1 Thessalonians 4:17, *harpagesometha* is translated as "caught up." There is a notion of a sudden swoop and a feeling of a force that cannot be resisted. Bible scholars generally agree that Paul's language in this passage requires a removal of believers from the earth at the time of Jesus' second coming.

Generally there are two main views concerning the relation of this event to the tribulation period which the prophetic Scriptures place immediately before the return of Christ. The first view is "pretribulation" which means that the church is raptured before the tribulation. Those holding this position believe that the divine wrath which is poured out on a Christ-rejecting society is not intended for the church and that God has promised to exempt the church from this whole period of trouble and judgment. Concerning the purpose of the tribulation Leon Wood writes:

> The twofold purpose of the tribulation is to punish the Gentile world for its sinfulness through past ages and to bring the nation of Israel to a frame of mind for receiving Christ as the Messiah-Deliverer. The church does not fit into this purpose in either respect, so that the absence of the church from the world would in no way hinder either goal being accomplished.[8]

Therefore the church is to be raptured from the earth prior to the tribulation. Those who hold this view believe that the church will not be found on earth during the tribulation.

A major weakness of this view is that it introduces a "secret coming" of Jesus for the church which cannot be supported in Scripture. Leon Wood believes that there will be two appearances of Christ separated "by no less than seven years."[9] John Walvoord plainly states that there will be two comings of Christ.

> The coming of Christ for His church is an event which takes place *before* the tribulation time while the coming of Christ to establish the Kingdom on earth occurs *after* the tribulation.[10]

This seven-year tribulation period has been identified by some as the seventieth week of Daniel's vision of the seventy weeks (Dan. 9:20–27). Those who hold to this position believe that the first sixty-nine weeks have been fulfilled with the first coming of Christ and the destruction of Jerusalem in A.D. 70. Between the first sixty-nine weeks and the seventieth week, an indefinite period of time exists, a period of time extending from Christ's first coming until the beginning of the tribulation. This period of time is the period in which we are now living, sometimes referred to as the "church age."

However, we find it difficult to believe that Daniel's seventy weeks can be divided up in this manner. Daniel was told that these seventy weeks would be divided up into three periods: a seven-week period, followed by a sixty-two week period, followed by one week. Each week would represent a period of seven years. Most Bible scholars agree that the first two of these periods occurred consecutively, and that they included happenings up to the time Jesus began his public ministry. Since period two followed period one without any intervening gap, and since there is nothing to indicate that there is a gap between period two and three, it is only logical to assume that period three followed consecutively after period two. There is no authority in Scripture for the assumption that Daniel's seventieth week is still in the future. The seventy weeks are to be seen as a symbolic number for the period that has been decreed for the accomplishment of God's work of salvation in Christ. The termination of the seventy weeks coincides with the first coming of Christ and his work for man's salvation and is not to be seen as the end of some future period. Nevertheless, as we have noted, there are those who see Daniel's seventieth week as the seven-year tribulation period marked off by two future appearances of Christ.

In turning to 1 Thessalonians 4:17, in which the rapture is specifically mentioned, we find no word of a secret coming of Christ for the church. Paul speaks of the Lord descending "from heaven with a cry of command, with the archangel's call, and with the sound of the trumpet of God" (1 Thess. 4:16). From Paul's use of language, one would hardly gather that Paul is describing a "secret coming" of the Lord for his church. It is my belief that pretribulationism is not taught in the New Testament. Rather, pretribulationism is an assumption in which Scripture is interpreted.

The second view is called posttribulationism. Those who hold to this position maintain that the church will remain on the earth during the predicted time of trouble and wrath. Jesus reminds the disciples that they are to expect suffering and persecution (Matt. 24:9ff; Mark 13:9ff; Luke 21:10ff). Although they will experience the tribulation they will be protected from the divine wrath by God (Rev. 7:1ff). Following the tribulation the church will be raptured from the earth to meet Christ. Those who hold this view believe that the Lord cannot be expected until the end of such a period. One would have to determine when the tribulation begins before he could anticipate the Lord's return.

A major weakness of this position lies in the fact that there are many New Testament passages which speak of the imminence of the Lord's return. The parables on watchfulness recorded in Matthew 24 and 25, while underscoring the element of preparedness or readiness, leave a rather overwhelming impression of imminence as well. In James 5:7-8 Christians are encouraged to be patient "for the coming of the Lord is at hand." In 1 Peter 4:7, there is the idea of the expected consummation of God's purpose: "The end of all things is at hand." The same idea is expressed by Paul in Philippians 4:5, "The Lord is at hand." Evidently some Christians in the Thessalonian church became convinced that the Lord's coming was so immediately imminent that they gave up work and became troublemakers in the church (2 Thess. 2:2; 3:6-12). Paul had to explain to them their misunderstanding of his teaching on the imminence of the Lord's return. It seems clear that these passages indicate that the New Testament does teach an imminent coming of Jesus Christ.

> The Bible teaches the coming of Christ as one glorious event, when the kingdom of this world is become the kingdom of our Lord and of His Christ. The Bible also teaches the coming of Christ as imminent, the "blessed hope" whose day and whose hour we know not, but that *could*, accordingly, be fulfilled at any hour.[11]

In summary, then, we may say that the rapture is essentially that event when living believers receive their resurrection bodies without passing through death. They are caught up from earth and along with the risen dead enter a new realm of glorified existence. This event will take place at the second coming and they will accompany him as he returns to earth. While the Scripture has much to say concerning Jesus Christ and his return, it has very little to say about the rapture as a unique event. The desire to see the Lord must not magnify what the New Testament says little about.

The Antichrist

In the discussion concerning the signs of Jesus' coming, we came to the conclusion that no matter how carefully we evaluate the signs and interpret history the coming of the end will be a surprise. There is one sign, however, which deserves some attention, the concept of the antichrist.

The term "antichrist" is found in the Bible only in the letters of John (1 John 2:18, 22; 4:3; 2 John 7). However, the idea behind this term is widespread. In the book of Daniel a rebellious power is symbolized in Daniel's little horn. In chapter seven the defeat of God's final enemy is pictured and in chapter eight Antiochus Epiphanes, the foreign ruler hated by the Jews because of his wickedness and religious persecution, is described. In Daniel 11 we have symbolized the "personification of evil" that has helped influence the New Testament concept of antichrist: (1) he eliminated the burnt offerings and defiled the Temple (Dan. 11:31; Matt. 24:15; Mark 13:14; Rev. 13:14-15); (2) he exalted himself to the position of deity (Dan. 11:36-39; 2 Thess. 2:8); (3) his death points to Christ's slaying of the "lawless one" (Dan. 11:45; 2 Thess. 2:8; Rev. 19:20). There also seems to be a relationship between the beast from the sea in Revelation 13:1 and the beasts in Daniel 7:3, 7. Whatever the basis for the beasts in Daniel, they clearly symbolize opposition toward God and his people.

As indicated earlier, the term "antichrist" only appears in the letters of John. The prefix *anti* has the meaning of "over against" or "in place of." The term antichrist then would mean that which is opposed to Christ, hence unlike Christ or that which takes Christ's place, hence a fake Christ, although both concepts may be present at the same time.

Jesus warns the disciples that in the last days "false Christs and false prophets will arise and show signs and wonders, to lead astray, if possible, the elect" (Mark 13:22; cf. Matt 24:24). Paul warns of the "son of perdition, who opposes and exalts himself against every so-called god or object of worship, so that he takes his seat in the temple of God, proclaiming himself to be God" (2 Thess. 2:3–5). He will be an agent of Satan, not Satan himself, with supernatural powers (2 Thess. 2:9). There seems to be no doubt in Paul's mind that he understood "the man of lawlessness," "the son of perdition" to be a historical person appearing in the last days. The characteristics of this personage are clear. He opposes God and exalts himself to a place of worship (2 Thess. 2:4), he claims supernatural power (2 Thess. 2:9), and he is recognized as the enemy of Christ (2 Thess. 2:8). He is the one who leads the great eschatological rebellion against God.

However, another concept emerges in the letters of John. John reminds his readers that it is the last hour and many antichrists have come (1 John 2:18). Later he states that the antichrist is one who denies that Jesus is the Christ (1 John 2:22; 4:3). In his second letter he states that many deceivers have gone out into the world denying the coming of Jesus in the flesh, "such a one is the deceiver and the antichrist" (2 John 7). John does not seem to be interested in a future individual. Rather his concern is to show that the spirit of the antichrist is at work in the present. This spirit denies that Jesus is the Christ. As far as John is concerned, whoever denies the Father and the Son is the antichrist (1 John 2:22). For John the importance of the incarnation was at stake. Jesus was indeed the very Christ of God come in the flesh. To deny this was to fall into the most serious error. The man who falls into this error and teaches that Jesus was not God in the flesh is not only a deceiver but the antichrist (2 John 7).

Finally, in the book of Revelation, the anti-Christian power is understood as being represented by the Roman State and its emperor worship (Rev. 13:1–10), and the antichrist also signifies the fake prophets who advocate this cult (Rev. 13:11–18). Many attempts have been made to identify the antichrist by decoding its number, 666. The early church identified the Roman emperors, especially Nero and Domitian, as the antichrist. John Hus and John Wyclif extended the idea of the antichrist to the whole catholic church. Martin Luther believed that the papacy was the antichrist. In contemporary history, Joseph Stalin and Adoph Hitler have been labeled as the antichrist. In light of the many interpretations of the antichrist, what shall we do with this concept?

We are not given a photograph-like representation of the antichrist in the New Testament. Rather, we are urged to a state of watchfulness. The antichrist, the many antichrists, the deceiver, the man of lawlessness: "the anti" assume many shapes depending upon times and circumstances. To calculate a name from the number 666 and thus identify the antichrist leads to numerous solutions. But perhaps these solutions are not what John had in mind. Perhaps we should understand the expression purely in terms of the symbolism of numbers. If we take the sum of the values represented by the letters of the name *Iesous,* the Greek name "Jesus," it comes to 888 (I=10, E=8, S=200, O=70, U=400, S=200). Each digit is one more than seven, the perfect number. But 666 yields the opposite picture, each digit falls one short. Thus, the number may not mean an individual, but a persistent falling short. The contrast between 666 and 888 conveys the difference between Satan's "christ" and God's Christ. The "christ" of Satan falls as far short of being the true deliverer as the Christ of God exceeds all the hopes of mankind for a redeemer. This may be the meaning of the phrase "it is a human number" (Rev. 13:18).

The most that we can say is that the antichrist is that power which seeks to dethrone God and to place itself on God's throne. Antichrist wears a mask of Christ and his kingdom is the counterfeit of truth. Antichrist is that power which looms up on the horizon of history, a universal power, showing no respect for boundaries. But one thing is clear, "the recognition of apostasy and antichrist is indeed possible, for the character of the 'anti' itself is clear: it is 'anti' the Lord."[12]

At this point I want to make a final statement as it relates to the subject of evil and the antichrist. A rash of demon-oriented motion pictures have flooded the American scene, i.e., *Rosemary's Baby, The Exorcist, The Omen,* as well as many others.

In *Rosemary's Baby* and *The Omen* a major theme is the birth of the antichrist and his future rise to power. In *The Exorcist* Satan emerges victorious because of the death of two priests. A common theme of these films, as well as many other demon-horror films, is that God is impotent or he is absent from the world. Satan is alive, well, and gaining in strength.

As a pastor, I am concerned about the possible influence these films may have on people. If one continues to feed his mind on the concept that God is impotent and Satan is strong, then the end result would be that evil will overcome us. These films also seem to imply that certain religious objects, e.g., holy water, a crucifix or cross, a Bible, or church buildings have some degree of power over evil. The biblical faith relative to salvation, that is, a personal trust in God through Jesus Christ, is replaced by faith in things for salvation.

As a pastor and as a student of the Bible I want to affirm that the whole witness of Scripture is that God is not impotent and that Satan is not supreme Lord of creation. The New Testament witness to Jesus Christ is one of victory over Satan. The major force of the teaching of the book of Revelation is that even though Satan is behind the trouble and evil in our world, God is still in ultimate control and that the day is coming when Satan and all evil will be destroyed. Let us take our cue from the teachings of the Bible and not from the films of Hollywood.

CHAPTER 7

The Millennium

One of the most intriguing and controversial questions of eschatology is the legitimacy of the expectation of a thousand year reign of Christ, the millennium. The only place in the Bible where the reign of Christ is called a millennium is mentioned in Revelation 20:2-6. Obviously one's view of the thousand years in Revelation 20 is intimately connected with the rest of his eschatology. If one expects a literal earthly reign of peace, then his interpretation of the present state of affairs will differ from that of someone who does not share such an expectation. This author does not accept the idea of a literal thousand year reign of peace because even in the regenerate the power of sin and death still operate. The Christian hope is not for a reign of peace in this dispensation, but for the resurrection and life eternal.

There are, however, three major views concerning the millennium. These three views to some degree base their position upon the passage in Revelation 20:2-6. We propose to do three things: first, highlight these three views; second, look at Revelation 20:2-6 and attempt to discern its meaning; and third, based on our findings, attempt an interpretation of this passage.

Premillennialism
The first view of the millennium to be considered is known as premillennialism. The view that this term expresses indicates

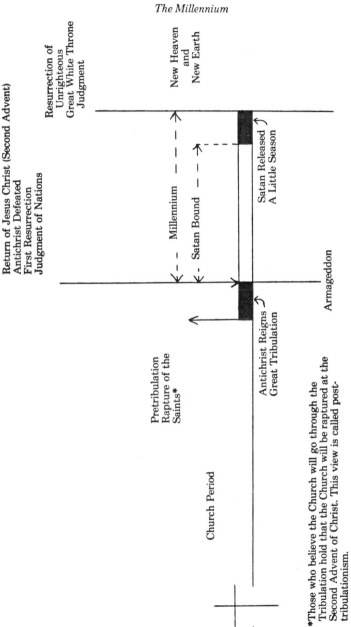

PREMILLENNIALISM

*Those who believe the Church will go through the Tribulation hold that the Church will be raptured at the Second Advent of Christ. This view is called post-tribulationism.

that the Lord will return before the millennium and establish it. While it is impossible to make a statement covering all the varieties of interpretation, an overall picture may be presented.

a. Before any final events of the second coming take place, living Christians will be "caught up" to meet the Lord. This is called the "secret" rapture. This is the position of those who believe that the saints will not go through the tribulation. There are other premillennialists who reject the idea of the secret rapture and hold that living Christians will be raptured at the public manifestation of Christ's second coming. Those who hold this position believe that the church will go through the tribulation.

b. At the return of Christ, the world will be under the sway of evil and antichrist will be in power.

c. At his coming Christ will defeat antichrist in an outstanding victory.

d. The resurrection of believers will occur either before the great tribulation (those holding a pretribulation view), or at the beginning of the millennium (the posttribulation view). The battle of Armageddon will bring the great tribulation to a climax.

e. At the beginning of the millennium there will be a preliminary judgment of the living nations. The risen saints will reign with Christ. Satan will be bound.

f. At the end of the millennium wickedness will break out, this being the result of Satan being freed. This "little season" is Satan's last attempt to defeat Jesus Christ.

g. After a short period the resurrection of the wicked will occur and this will be followed by the last judgment at the great white throne.

The preceding series of events represents the premillennial view of eschatology. Those who teach do so on the understanding that just as the Old Testament is preparatory for the church period so the millennial period is preparatory for the eternal state. The millennium then is that period in which God's kingdom is seen in its public and glorious manisfestation just prior to the eternal state. There is, however, a second form of premillennialism that is called "dispensationalism." Dispensationalism teaches that the millennium is the period in which God will fulfill all of the promises made to Israel in the Old Testament. Dispensationalists believe that when Israel rejected Christ as King, the covenant made between David and God was not annulled. They believe that the covenant remains intact regardless of whether or not Israel rejected or accepted Christ. The period in which these promises will be fulfilled is the millennium.

> The great truth of the millennium is that all these promises will be fulfilled, because then true allegiance will be rendered to the King. Israel will become the leading nation of the world, her borders will stretch from Egypt to the Euphrates, and she will be the influence and world-wide blessing predicted.[1]

The basis of the dispensational approach to interpreting prophecy is what some call "consistent literalism." We have discussed some weaknesses of this approach in Chapter 3. Another weakness of this approach is highlighted by C. Norman Kraus in his book, *Dispensationalism In America*:

> The dispensationalist interpretation is built on an inadequate concept of the nature of language and its use. In seeking to uphold the supernatural quality of the Biblical narrative it has assumed that the Biblical language is like the language of a science textbook; that is, that its terms have a fixed meaning from beginning to end.[2]

This method of biblical interpretation by dispensationalists tends to make one a slave of the letter and even has the tendency to mark insignificant details and elevate them beyond their meaning by the biblical writers.

Postmillennialism

A second view of the millennium is called postmillennialism. This term describes a view which places the coming of Christ after the millennium. A picture of this view is something like the following:

a. In the present world order, good and evil continue together.

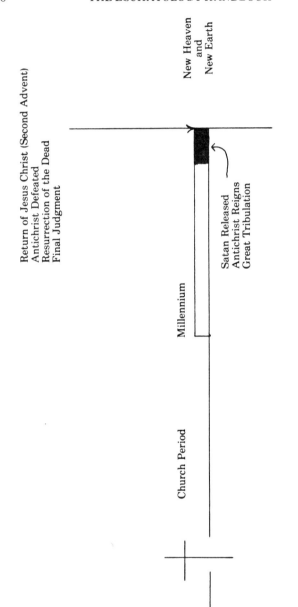

Return of Jesus Christ (Second Advent)
Antichrist Defeated
Resurrection of the Dead
Final Judgment

New Heaven
and
New Earth

Armageddon

Satan Released
Antichrist Reigns
Great Tribulation

Millennium

Church Period

POSTMILLENNIALISM

b. In the latter days under the power of the Holy Spirit, the work of God becomes greatly revived and believers shall become aware of their spiritual strength that to a degree unknown they shall overpower the forces of evil.

c. Following this "golden age" of the church, the millennium, a brief apostasy will occur—a terrible conflict between the forces of evil and good. This is the time when Satan will be released, antichrist comes to power, and the great tribulation takes place. The battle of Armageddon will bring the great tribulation to a close at the time of Christ's return.

d. Christ will return, the dead will be raised, and the final judgment will take place.

Objections to this view can be summed up in three statements. First, there is no ground in Scripture for the hope of unparalleled spiritual prosperity just before the return of Christ. Second, the concept of the passing of the present age into a "golden age" of the future is contradicted by the increase of wickedness prophesied in Scripture. Third, this view simply is contrary to what the Bible has to say concerning man and his sinful nature.

Amillennialism

A third view of the millennium is called amillennialism. Those who hold this position do so on the basis that there is no sufficient ground for the expectation of a literal thousand year period of time. Amillennialists cannot find any place in Scripture that specifically states that a thousand year period will follow the Lord's return, for the second advent immediately ushers in the last judgment and the eternal state. An amillennial picture of eschatological events takes the following shape.

a. The end of the age will be marked by increasing lawlessness and godlessness.

b. This lawlessness and godlessness will reach its climax in the appearance of the antichrist. Satan will seem to gain strength as he recruits the forces of evil for one last attempt to destroy Jesus Christ. The "great tribulation" will be brought to a climax by the battle of Armageddon.

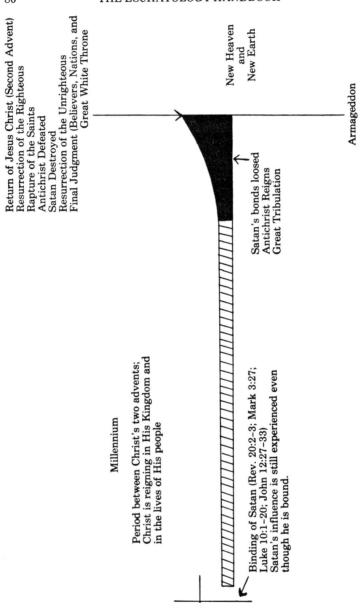

Return of Jesus Christ (Second Advent)
Resurrection of the Righteous
Rapture of the Saints
Antichrist Defeated
Satan Destroyed
Resurrection of the Unrighteous
Final Judgment (Believers, Nations, and
    Great White Throne

New Heaven
and
New Earth

Satan's bonds loosed
Antichrist Reigns
Great Tribulation

Millennium

Period between Christ's two advents;
Christ is reigning in His Kingdom and
in the lives of His people

Binding of Satan (Rev. 20:2–3; Mark 3:27;
Luke 10:1–20; John 12:27–33)
Satan's influence is still experienced even
though he is bound.

Armageddon

AMILLENNIALISM

c. Christ will return in glory accompanied by the resurrected saints and those who "are alive and remain" will be caught up to join the redeemed host.

d. The second coming of Christ will destroy the evil world.

e. The resurrection of the wicked and the last judgment synchronize with the second coming of Christ.

f. The present earth will pass away and a new heaven and a new earth will take its place.

Amillennialism rests on a symbolic interpretation of Revelation 20 which gives full value to the apocalyptic nature of the book. The thousand years is understood consistently with the symbolic use of numbers in apocalyptic language. Objections to the concept of amillennialism all stem from one basic root, that is, the difficulty which some biblical expositors have in accepting the symbolic nature of Revelation 20.

The key biblical passage is Revelation 20:2-6 where the thousand year period is marked off by two decisive moments, the binding of Satan and his release. This period, the millennium, exists between the binding of Satan and his release and consists of the reign of the believers with Christ. The word *chilias* means "a thousand." This word appears in Revelation 20:2, 3, 4, 5, 6, 7. In what sense is this word used in this passage?

Some believe that John used numbers not necessarily to mark a definite duration of time but rather as an expression of the quality of time in reference to history. The number one thousand qualifies a critical part of God's action with men. The number one thousand does not involve any kind of statement about the duration of the manifestation of Jesus' victory on the old earth. The millennium then is to be understood as the final phase and full revelation of God's kingdom which was inaugurated in the person and work of Jesus Christ. In his study of the book of Revelation, Thomas Torrance writes:

> Extraordinary symbols have been thrown upon the screen of vision, strange uncanny creatures in fantastic mixture of the mythical and the recognizable, and now on the same screen of vision we have the symbol of a thousand years. It is quite evi-

dent that we have no more right to take this thousand years literally than we have to take the ten-headed and seven-horned monster literally. It is entirely out of place therefore to bring down the thousand years out of its apocalyptic setting and place it on the ordinary plane of history, as if it could be handled by a worldly arithmetic and manipulated in calculations about the dispensations of time or about the end of the world.[3]

Others believe that the millennium does not represent a period of time before or after the coming of Christ. The number one thousand is to be understood as an idea of completeness. The millennium then is the picture of those who suffered and died for Christ and now reigning with him, "a picture of perfect blessedness." John used the figure of a thousand years to show the character of God's "rest" for mankind rather than a duration of time. Despite the persecution of believers, Christ is not defeated, nor are those who have died for his sake. Our glimpse behind the scenes shows us martyrs reigning and Satan bound. In a sense then, the millennium is simply an image used to picture the completion of God's redemptive process in history.

There are those who interpret the millennium as a literal period of time.

It is difficult to understand the thousand years for which he [Satan] was bound with strict literalness in view of the obvious symbolic use of numbers in the Revelation. A thousand equals the third power of ten—an ideal time. While we need not take it literally, the thousand years does appear to represent a real period of time, however long or short it may be.[4]

Others believe that millennium is to be a period of one thousand years. The thousand years then are to be understood in their literal sense. Dispensationalists believe that the basic purpose of the millennium is to have a period when God's authority will be recognized in all the earth. This earth is to be one thousand years in duration. Leon Wood, a dispensationalist, states that,

Though this figure is used in Scripture only here [Rev. 20:1-7], its manner of usage makes the literal intention unmistakable. It is mentioned no less than six times, and each time it is in reference to a distinct feature of that period. The force of this is to say, in six different ways, that the duration will indeed be of this length.[5]

Does the vision of Revelation 20 intend to sketch for us a particular phase of history? A choice must be made whether this vision does indeed intend to portray a literal future reign on earth or whether this vision is the

> ... apocalyptic unveiling of the reality of salvation in Christ as a backdrop to the reality of the suffering and martyrdom that still continue as long as the dominion of Christ remains hidden.[6]

A choice for the latter would be in harmony with the contrast between the crucifixion and resurrection of Jesus and his second coming. In symbolic terms those who have suffered and died for Christ are seen to be made alive to reign with Christ. When the vision speaks of the release of Satan, the intent is to show the victory of Christ and the ultimate impotence of the power of Satan, not to predict a chronologically long and difficult time. In visionary terms John reveals how powerless Satan really is, how short the time of his freedom (Rev. 20:3), how really minor his war, how foolish in the face of Christ and his victory. Revelation is not a discourse about the future to satisfy our curiosity but an affirmation that proclaims the incontrovertible salvation of God. Its message is not only oriented to the present but points to the future. It is a view of reality seen in eschatological perspective in the last days. Revelation is not the riddle of history but the book of God's solution to history.

I do not believe in a literal millennium of a thousand years duration. The "thousand years" mentioned in Revelation 20:4-6 is a real number used as an apocalyptic symbol of the fullness of time that has broken into our world in the person of Jesus Christ. The millennium represents a real period of time between the first advent of our Lord and his second coming. Its duration is known only to God since its consummation will occur at the return of Jesus Christ. "But of that day or that hour no one knows, not even the angels in heaven, nor the Son, but only the Father" (Mark 13:32).

Does the rejection of the certainty of a literal millennium weaken eschatological expectation? We believe not. Certainty is denied to us in any attempt to calculate the date of Jesus' return. This does not lessen eschatological expectation, but stimulates it. Faith is always thrown back to the idea that God's ways remain and will remain inscrutable. This does not mean we go blindly toward the future. As we approach that day our eyes are opened. Still, we "see in a mirror dimly" (1 Cor. 13:12).

CHAPTER 8

The Resurrection

The most startling characteristic of the first Christian preaching was the emphasis on the resurrection of Jesus Christ (e.g., Acts 2:23-24, 32; 3:14-15; 4:10; 10:39-40; 13:28-31; 17:2-3, 16-32). The first Christian community was absolutely certain that Jesus was raised from the dead. The apostle Paul affirmed that the Christian faith stands or falls on the reality of the resurrection of Jesus Christ from the dead (1 Cor. 15: 12-19). It has been said that "a Christian faith that is not resurrection faith can therefore be called neither Christian nor faith."[1] The expectation of the resurrection in the New Testament rests in a promise inseparable from the salvation already granted in Christ. It is seen as rooted in an immovable foundation.

There is little in the Old Testament about the doctrine of resurrection. The men of the Old Testament were practical men concentrating on the task of living out the present life, and they had little time to develop concepts about life after death. Nevertheless a hope developed that death was not the end of personal existence. The Psalmist, torn by the inequities of experience, affirms his confidence:

> For thou dost not give me up to Sheol,
> or let thy godly one see the Pit.

Thou dost show me the path of life;
  in thy presence there is fulness of joy,
  in thy right hand are pleasures for evermore.

(Ps. 16:10-11)

But God will ransom my soul from the power of Sheol,
  for he will receive me.

(Ps. 49:15)

Nevertheless I am continually with thee;
  thou dost hold my right hand.
Thou dost guide me with thy counsel,
  and afterward thou wilt receive me to glory.
Whom have I in heaven but thee?
  And there is nothing upon earth that I desire besides thee.
My flesh and my heart may fail,
  but God is the strength of my heart and my portion for ever.

(Ps. 73:23-26)

And Job, after experiencing sickness, suffering, and the loss of all material things, can still affirm:

For I know that my Redeemer lives,
  and at last he will stand upon the earth;
and after my skin has thus been destroyed,
  then from my flesh I shall see God,

(Job 19:25-26)

In the Old Testament victory over death by resurrection becomes clear in two passages, Isaiah 26:19 and Daniel 12:2-3. In Isaiah 26:19 the prophet announces that the Lord's righteous will be raised from the dead. No such hope is held out for the unrighteous (Isa. 26:14). Daniel 12:2-3 states that the resurrection will include both the righteous and the unrighteous. The author seems to have felt God must do justice on the one hand to the martyrs for the faith and on the other to the apostates. This passage states that where reward or punishment are deserved, the dead should arise to receive them. The God of justice will bring justice to all his people. If redemption is to have complete victory over sin and death, then there must ultimately be the sure hope of a resurrection from the dead.

The New Testament bears witness to that which was hoped for in the Old Testament.

Only in the New Testament is the meaning of the reality of Yahweh's power of life fully revealed. The focus is no longer on what God *can do*, but on what He *has done*. All the earlier incidental and fragmented references to resurrection center in the fact of salvation through the actual resurrection of Jesus Christ, the first-born from the dead.[2]

The resurrection of Jesus Christ was a new reality breaking through into this world and offering the promise and guarantee of future salvation. It was an event which took place at a certain time, in a certain place, in the context of human history. It is concrete, it has a character which is personal, historic, and written within space and time.

The Resurrection of Jesus

The word most commonly used to express the idea of the resurrection is *anastasis,* which is derived from the verb *anistemi.* The verb *anistemi* means to raise, to erect, to raise up. The noun *anastasis,* then, means rise or resurrection, which has the sense of standing up or a state of standing again. Another word used in the New Testament to convey the idea of rising from the dead is *egeiro.* This word means to awaken, to raise up, or to bring into being. In New Testament usage, whenever these words are used in relation to a body, it means the raising of the body, the return of the body from the grip of death. Resurrection then is "the raising up of the body so that it is released from the powers of death and made to live, to stand up again."[3]

In the New Testament the idea and hope of resurrection centers in the resurrection of Jesus. The Gospels record that on three occasions Jesus brought back people from the powers of death; the son of the widow of Nain (Luke 7:11–17), the daughter of Jairus (Matt. 9:18–19, 23–26; Mark 5:22–24, 35–43; Luke 8:40–42, 49–56), and Lazarus (John 11:17–44). However, these were not resurrections but resuscitations. The dead were brought to a physical, mortal existence, and presumably, after a normal span of years, succumbed again to death. But not so with Jesus. His resurrection means that death is abolished and that life is brought to light in the gospel (2 Tim. 1:10).

The Gospels also tells us that Jesus tried to prepare the disciples for his death and subsequent resurrection. He predicted his death and resurrection (Matt. 16:21; 17:23; 20:19; Mark 8:31; 9:31; 10:34; Luke 9:22; 18:33). In John 2:19 Jesus referred to his resurrection by saying, "Destroy this temple, and in three days I will raise it up."

It must be emphasized that Jesus' resurrection was not a resuscitation, that is, a return to physical, mortal life. Rather, Jesus' resurrection was one of glory instead of the weakness of physical existence. Paul's encounter with the resurrected Lord on the road to Damascus Road (Acts 9:1–9; 22:6–11; 26:12–18) convinced him that Jesus' resurrection was fact not fiction. Jesus appeared to Paul in a manifestation of brilliance and glory and out of this brilliance of light came a voice which identified itself as Jesus. Thus Paul could state that "Christ was raised from the dead by the glory of the Father" (Rom. 6:4).

The resurrection appearance of Jesus in the Gospels appears to be of a different kind. Matthew records that as the women were leaving the empty tomb Jesus met them "and they came up and took hold of his feet and worshipped him" (Matt. 28:9). In Mark's Gospel (Mark 16:9–20) there is an emphasis on the fact that Jesus rose bodily from the dead. Luke records that two disciples on the road to Emmaus recognized Jesus in the act of breaking bread (Luke 24:30–31). Furthermore, Luke records Jesus telling his disciples to touch his body so that they could assure themselves that what they were seeing was not a ghost (Luke 24:39). John states that Jesus' risen body could be touched (20:17) and seen (20:19–29). The story of doubting Thomas indicates that Thomas was invited by Jesus to put his hand in the wound of Jesus' hands and spear thrust in his side (John 20:24–29).

The point is that while Paul's encounter was with the glorified Christ, the Gospels emphasize Jesus' bodily resurrection. One way to harmonize these accounts is to state that Jesus was glorified, not at the resurrection, but at the time of his as-

cension. This is certainly possible. However, it is also possible
to affirm that Jesus rose from the grave in his glorified body,
that he appeared in this glory to Paul, but that his appearance
recorded in the Gospels are condescension to the earthbound
senses of the disciples. It must be noted that in spite of Jesus'
predictions of his death and resurrection the disciples were not
expecting to see Jesus alive after his crucifixion.

The three facts which emerge from the accounts in the Gospels are these: *Identity*: the resurrected Jesus was the same
Jesus who was crucified. *Continuity*: Jesus was raised in bodily form which was capable of making an impact on the physical senses. Paul thus affirms the bodily nature of the resurrection (1 Cor. 15). *Discontinuity*: while Jesus was raised in
bodily form, it was not the same body prior to his crucifixion.
Jesus' resurrection body was a transformed body which possessed new powers (Luke 24:31, 36; John 20:19, 26). Jesus' resurrection body was one which was not subject to the laws of
space and time or dependent upon nature.

Now it may seem to the reader that we are spending too
much time on an exposition of Jesus' resurrection body when
our concern is the eschatological resurrection of persons at the
end of the age. The reason for this is that the resurrection of
Jesus is itself an eschatological event. Jesus' resurrection is
not an isolated event in history but is itself the beginning of
the eschatological resurrection. Jesus is called the "first-born
from the dead" (Col. 1:18). This means that Jesus was not only
the first to rise from the dead but that he stands at the head of
resurrection life. The eschatological nature of Christ's resurrection is also seen in Paul's statement that Jesus' resurrection was "the first fruits of those who have fallen asleep"
(1 Cor. 15:20). This means at least two things. *First*, the resurrection of Jesus Christ guarantees the resurrection of believers.
Resurrection becomes more than a hope, it becomes an event.
And, the resurrection of believers is dependent upon Christ's
resurrection (1 Cor. 15:14–18). *Second*, Christ as first fruits of
the resurrection tells us that our resurrection will be like his.
When Christ comes in power and glory, he "will change our

lowly body to be like his glorious body, by the power which enables him even to subject all things to himself" (Phil. 3:21).

The question now is, "What kind of a body will we have in the resurrection?" The next section will give an answer to this question.

The Resurrection of the Righteous

The general New Testament position is that the resurrection of Jesus Christ carries with it the promise of the resurrection of believers. Jesus said, "I am the resurrection and the life; he who believes in me, though he die, yet shall he live, and whoever lives and believes in me shall never die" (John 11:25-26). On several other occasions he spoke of raising believers up on the last day (John 6:39, 40, 44, 54). Peter affirms that by the resurrection of Jesus Christ believers have been given a "living hope" that one day they too shall be raised to an "inheritance which is imperishable, undefiled, and unfading" (1 Peter 1:3-4). This hope is for "adoption as sons, the redemption of our bodies" (Rom. 8:23). Nowhere in the gospel of Christ is salvation portrayed as the soul's liberation from the body. When Paul says, "We wait for adoption as sons" (Rom. 8:23), he adds, "the redemption of our bodies," not "the redemption from our bodies." Thus, in the New Testament, the resurrection of the body is seen as the consummation of hope and the completion of the redemptive process begun by faith in Christ.

There are several passages in the New Testament which are basic to the Christian perspective of the resurrection. While these passages touch on a number of Jesus' teachings, attention will be restricted only to what they say concerning resurrection.

In John 5:28-29, Jesus says that the time is coming when the dead will be raised, both the righteous and the unrighteous. This statement of Jesus implies that there will be one general resurrection at the last day. At the consummation of the age the voice of the Son will usher in the resurrection. All the dead will rise. Jesus' statement in this passage provides no basis whatever for the idea that there will be two separate resurrections at two different periods of time. The contrast in this passage is not between two different times when men are to be raised but between the different kinds of men who are to be raised. Jesus' teaching here refers to nothing short of the resurrection of the body.

In one of his letters to the Thessalonian Christians, Paul speaks a word about the relationship of the Christian dead to the return of the Lord (1 Thess. 4:13-18). Paul assures them that the resurrection of Jesus Christ is an indication that the bonds of death have been broken and that ultimately death itself will be totally destroyed (1 Thess. 4:14). What Paul is saying is that those who are living when Christ returns will have no advantage over those who have died. At the return of Christ the "dead in Christ will rise first; then we who are alive, who are left, shall be caught up together with them in the clouds to meet the Lord in the air" (1 Thess. 4:16-17). In this passage, Paul was not concerned about giving a detailed program of activity in relationship to the Lord's return. Paul says nothing about the resurrection of the unbelievers, nothing about judgment, and there is no indication in this passage of two resurrections. Paul's intention was to comfort the Thessalonian Christians by assuring them that at Christ's second coming, they will be caught up to meet the Lord and those who were raised at the Lord's return.

In Paul's letter to the Corinthian church, he answers the question, "How are the dead raised and with what kind of body?" (1 Cor. 15:35). Paul's answer to the question, "How are the dead raised?" is simply that the resurrection comes through God's power. Paul illustrates this first by saying that a seed is sown and buried. It dies, but it is raised up with a new and more glorious body. He then goes on to say that there are different kinds of bodies, one for men, another for animals, another for fish and birds. Paul continues by saying that there is a difference between celestial and terrestrial bodies, as well as a difference between the glory of different celestial bodies. What Paul is saying is that as God has the power and wisdom to give the kind of bodies needed for earthly life, so he has the power and wisdom to give the kind of body that will be needed on the eternal and spiritual level of life.

Paul now answers the question as to the nature of the resurrection body (1 Cor. 15:42-50). Paul uses four contrasts to show the difference between the body that dies and the body that is raised from the dead (1 Cor. 15:42-44). This leads Paul to say, "If there is a physical body, there is also a spiritual body" (1 Cor. 15:44). Paul saw the resurrection body as a body that is real, but not one restored to its former limited physical nature and function. It will be a spiritual body, an expression of man's whole self, continuous with his earthly body but different from it. To clarify his position Paul relates the concept of the body to man's relationship to Adam and to Christ. Out of his relationship to Adam man has a physical body that is subject to decay and to death. Out of his relationship to Christ the believer is to have a spiritual body that is not subject to decay. The resurrection body of Christ shows us something of what life will be like for believers in that new world which their resurrection will usher in.

Paul concludes his remarks (1 Cor. 15:51-58) by stating that those who rise will not be creatures of flesh and blood. Rather they will be raised with bodies no longer liable to death and decay. Those who are alive will be transformed, receiving their spiritual bodies. The resurrection of the dead is to occur at the second coming of Jesus (1 Cor. 15:52; cf. 1 Thess. 4:16) at which time the living believers will be transformed almost immediately. Both the dead in Christ and those believers who are living will be transformed at the second coming of Jesus. The result of this resurrection is that death has been robbed of its victory over man. Through the redemptive work of God in Christ, both sin and death have been defeated (1 Cor. 15:54-57).

The Christian believer does not have to ask if there will be a resurrection for him, for he is assured of his resurrection by the promises given in the New Testament. Jesus promised that those who believe in him will be raised on the last day (John 6:39, 40, 44, 54) and that they will never die (John 11:25-26). Peter assures believers that their hope for resurrection is based on Jesus' resurrection from the dead (1 Peter 1:3-4). Paul argues that if Christ had not been raised, then our faith is vain; but since Christ has been raised from the dead, then at his coming all who believe in him will also be raised from the dead (1 Cor. 15:12-14, 20-23). Believers are assured that "he who raised the Lord Jesus will raise us also with Jesus" (2 Cor. 4:14).

The nature of the believer's resurrection body has already been indicated in principle. In Philippians 3:21 Paul assures the believer that when Christ returns, he will "change our lowly body to be like his glorious body." Commenting on this passage, J. A. Schep states that "since this glorious body of our Lord . . . is a glorified body of *flesh*, the resurrection-body of the believer can be none other than a similar body of *flesh.*"⁴ We shall ". . . bear the image of the man of heaven" (1 Cor. 15:49), ". . . we shall be like him, for we shall see him as he is" (1 John 3:2). The resurrection of believers means that the whole man, who has really died, is recalled to life by a new act of creation by God.

Paul states that the resurrection body of the believer will in some way be similar to his earthly body (1 Cor. 15:36-38). As each kind of seed brings forth its own kind of plant, so the individual body will be raised in such a way that its individuality will be preserved. There is a new and different body but the same person. What is vital to a person as a person will be raised in a spiritual body. There is a continuity between what dies and what is raised because it is the person who is buried and raised. But there is also a discontinuity in the sense that the same physical body will not be raised. The same person will be raised in a new spiritual body created by God for life in the "new earth and the new heavens."

For the believer, the resurrection of the body means that he will join the fellowship of the saints, the redeemed, in the service, praise, and worship of God. Death has been conquered, the last enemy defeated, and he can say with Paul, "Thanks be to God, who gives us the victory through our Lord Jesus Christ" (1 Cor. 15:57).

The Resurrection of the Unrighteous

Not all who will be raised on the last day will be raised to blessing. Jesus speaks of "the resurrection of life": but also of "the resurrection of judgment" (John 5:29). The teaching of the New Testament indicates that all will be raised on the last day, but that those who have rejected Christ will find the resurrection a serious matter indeed.

It must be noted at this point that not all students of the Bible believe in teaching of a literal eternal judgment. Those who hold this view teach a doctrine called universalism. This doctrine essentially teaches that all men are God's children and that God will not rest until all men are saved. A brief description of this doctrine and a response to it will be given in the chapter dealing with one's eternal destiny.

The future nature of the resurrection is specifically related by Paul to the time of the second coming of Christ. In 1 Thessalonians 4:13-18 the resurrection will become reality when the Lord returns. In 1 Corinthians 15:35-58 Paul argues that the resurrection will occur at the second coming of Christ. In 2 Thessalonians 1:7 Paul relates the consummation of resurrection and judgment to the second advent of Christ. The second advent is called a "revelation" also in 1 Corinthians 1:7, and the first epistle of Peter (1:7, 13; 4:13). Involved in it are the "revelations" of the sons of God (Rom. 8:19) and of his righteous judgment (Rom. 2:5). In John 5:28-29 Jesus states that both the righteous and the unrighteous will be raised at his return.

Are the righteous and the unrighteous to be raised at the same time? Those who hold to the dispensational view say no. They believe that the righteous and the unrighteous will not be raised at the same time. Since their destinies are not the same their resurrections cannot be at the same time. The righteous are raised before the millennium and the unrighteous are raised after the millennium. Two men who represent this viewpoint state the dispensational position clearly. Leon Wood in *The Bible and Future Events,* states, "The second resurrection occurs after the millennium and will include the unsaved of all ages."[5] John Walvoord in *The Return of the Lord* states that,

"The wicked dead will not be raised until the end of the millennium in contrast to the resurrected saints who will reign with the Lord for a thousand years."[6]

The key passage is Revelation 20:4-6. Those who hold the doctrine of two resurrections say this passage teaches that the righteous will be raised at one time and the unrighteous at another. The expression in the last part of verse 5, "the first resurrection," refers to the resurrection of the righteous, and the expression in the first part of verse 5, "the rest of the dead," refers to the resurrection of the unrighteous at the end of the millennium. Part of the problem is that this is the only place in the New Testament where two resurrections are mentioned. However, this does not mean that the doctrine is to be ruled out on this basis. One clear statement in the New Testament that the righteous are raised at one time and the unrighteous a thousand years later would be sufficient. But there is no such statement in the New Testament, and Revelation 20:4-6 can hardly be called clear on this point.

In Revelation 20:4-6 the first resurrection refers to the triumph of the martyrs, while the "second resurrection," which is not mentioned but implied, must be the general resurrection discussed so often in the New Testament. The "first death," which is not mentioned but implied, means physical death, while the term "second death," which is mentioned, is symbolic of eternal separation, eternal punishment in the lake of fire.

The meaning of Revelation 20:4-6 is to be found in a synthesis of both the symbolic and of the literal. The terms "first resurrection" and "second death" are both symbolic while "second resurrection" and "first death" which are implied and not mentioned are to be understood as literal. The New Testament teaches that at Christ's second coming the dead will be raised. The New Testament also teaches that physical death will be a separation, a condition of being cut off from life as we experienced it. John uses the term "first resurrection" to describe the experiences of the martyrs. The term "second death" is used by John as a symbol of the eternal separation from the blessings and fellowship with God. The contrast between the literal and symbolic is shown below:

The "first resurrection" is a symbol of the triumph of the martyrs.	The "second resurrection" (not mentioned but implied) is the general resurrection.
The "first death" (not mentioned but implied) is physical death.	The "second death" is symbolic of eternal separation from God.

In verse 4 John describes the victory of the martyrs who lost their lives in Christ's service. They are seen, not as being defeated, but as reigning with Christ. The second death has no claim upon them. Christ promises a share in God's kingdom to all who overcome (Rev. 2:26-28; 3:12, 21). We see no reason to limit this promise only to the martyrs. The promise of reigning with Christ is again repeated in Revelation 5:9-10, and it is addressed to all the saints. Therefore, while John singles out the martyrs for special mention, Revelation 20:4-6 promises victory to all Christians who remain faithful in Christ's service.

Other Bible students agree that Revelation 20:4-6 teaches two resurrections, but they are a spiritual resurrection and a physical resurrection. Those who hold this understanding believe that the New Testament teaches a spiritual resurrection alongside a physical resurrection.

Everyone who is "born again" (John 3:3-8) has already experienced a spiritual resurrection. In Ephesians 2:1-6 Paul clearly teaches that we, who once were dead in sins, have been made alive and have been raised from the dead with Jesus Christ. This same thought is also expressed in Colossians 2:13; 3:1; and 1 John 3:14. The emphasis is clearly a resurrection of the spirit which occurs when one comes to faith in Jesus Christ.

In John 5:24-29 Jesus speaks of two resurrections, a spiritual resurrection and a physical resurrection. These are the only two types of resurrections ever mentioned by Jesus. An examination of this passage indicates the characteristics of these two resurrections.

a. One is present (5:25 "now is"); the other is future (5:28-29 "is coming").
b. One is spiritual (5:24-25); the other is physical (5:28-29).
c. One is restricted to believers (5:24-25); the other includes everyone (5:28-29 "all").

In this passage it is stated that there is first a spiritual resurrection to be followed by an eschatological bodily resurrection. In other words, there takes place in the Christian a real resurrection. He dies with Christ when his old life is crucified and he is raised to new life in Christ becoming a new creature (Rom. 6:3-11; 2 Cor. 5:17).

In summary, it seems that the idea of two resurrections, one for the righteous separated by a thousand years from the one for the unrighteous, is not well grounded in Scripture. It is, of course, quite possible that there will be two tempos in the resurrection, and that the resurrection of the righteous will slightly precede that of the unrighteous. But this does not change the fact that, generally speaking, the resurrection of both the righteous and the unrighteous will occur at the second coming of Jesus Christ. The outcome of the resurrection will be different for each group, but it does not mean that one will be separated from the other by a thousand years. Two of the most specific passages about the resurrection are Daniel 12:2 and John 5:28-29 which were previously discussed. In neither of these passages is there any indication of two separate resurrections separated by a thousand-year millennium. The New Testament knows only of one bodily resurrection, that of both the righteous and the unrighteous at the second coming of the Lord.

CHAPTER 9

The Judgment

There is, to be sure, a sense in which people are judged already in this present life, by the response they make to Jesus Christ (John 3:18-21; see also John 3:36, 5:24). In other words a divine judgment rests upon those who refuse to believe in Christ. But the Bible also speaks of a final judgment at the end of history, in which all persons will appear before the judgment seat of Christ. It is this final judgment that we will discuss in this chapter.

Some Christians would regard a final judgment as unnecessary since the destiny of each person is determined by his response to Jesus Christ by the time of death. In an earlier chapter we discussed the doctrine of the intermediate state. It was discovered that when a Christian dies, he or she is saved and will immediately after death be at home with the Lord. If however, a person dies in unbelief, he or she is lost and will go immediately to a place of separation from God, a place of agony and torment. If this is true, then why a final judgment? It is true that such a judgment would be necessary for those still living at Christ's return, but not for those who died.

This objection to a final judgment is based on the assumption that the final judgment is to determine a person's future destiny. But this assumption is incorrect. By the time of final judgment the future destiny of all persons will be determined. A person's future destiny is determined by one's response either for or against Christ (John ?:16-18, 36; 5:24, 26-29). From John 10:27-28 we learn that Christ knows his followers and has given them eternal life, so that no one can snatch them out of his hand (see also Rom. 8:1-4, 31-39).

What then is the purpose of a final judgment? *First,* the final judgment will display the sovereignty of God and the glory of God. Up to this point the destiny of each person was hidden, now that destiny will be revealed, along with the faith each one had or did not have, and the life each one lived. God's grace will be magnified in the salvation of his people, and God's justice will be realized in the condemnation of his enemies. What is central then in the final judgment is not the destinies of individuals but the glory of God. *Second,* the final judgment will reveal the degree of reward and the degree of punishment each one shall receive. Each person must stand before God (Rom. 2:5-10; 14:10) and give an account of his life (2 Cor. 5:10). Christians need to remember that they will stand before God, and even though their salvation is secure, they could lose some rewards (1 Cor. 3:13-15). *Third,* the final judgment will be the time when God grants divine approval to the choices a person makes, either for or against Christ. God will assign to each person the place where he will spend eternity.

God's final judgment is assumed in the Bible. There is an abundance of Scripture passages that support the assumption. Many of these passages are not presented to prove the fact of judgment but to warn people of its reality and its coming While there are many illustrations of judgment in the New Testament, there are three basic pictures or concepts of judgment presented: the sheep and goat judgment (Matt. 25:31-46); the judgment seat of Christ (Rom. 14:10; 2 Cor. 5:10); and the great white throne judgment (Rev. 20:11-15).

Do these speak of three separate judgments or are they different ways of looking at one judgment to come at the end of the world? There are some who believe that these are different judgments, taking place at different times, for different purposes, and with reference to different people. The sheep and goat judgment will take place on earth and is God's judgment upon the nations to determine which nations shall continue in the world during the millennium. The judgment seat of Christ takes place in heaven during the seven years of the great tribulation on the earth and is a judgment on believers. The great white throne judgment takes place in the air while the earth is being purged by fire at the end of the millennium and is judgment upon the wicked of all the ages. A look at these three passages is necessary before we continue the discussion on the subject of judgment.

The sheep and goat judgment is an illustration Jesus used in answering the question of the disciples about the destruction of Jerusalem, the second coming of Christ, and the end of the world (Matt. 25:31-46). This illustration is a description of the last judgment. The separation that takes place in this passage is a separation of men. The expression "all the nations" is used to indicate the universal nature of the judgment. It is to be noted that the essence of the passage is that the ultimate test of relationship to Christ is the test of life and love. In ministering to the needy, one ministers to Christ. The contrasting fates are eternal life for the righteous and eternal punishment for the unrighteous. The division and sentence are final. We believe that any attempt to limit the time of punishment is misguided; the same adjective "eternal" is used to describe the everlasting duration of both the punishment and life. There is nothing to suggest anything other than that in each usage the same meaning is intended. This judgment takes place "when the Son of man comes in his glory" (Matt. 25:31). This implies that the judgment will take place at the return of the Lord.

In Romans 14:10 and in 2 Corinthians 5:10, Paul uses the term "judgment seat" before which all will appear. The word *"bema"* means step, stride, tribunal, a judicial bench, or speaker's platform. The word *bema* is used twelve times in the New Testament (Matt. 27:19; John 19:13; Acts 7:5; 12:21; 18:12, 16-17; 25:6, 10, 17; Rom. 14:10; 2 Cor. 5:10), and its usage simply means a place of the exercising of authority or judgment. In Romans 14:10, Paul is reminding those with a judgmental attitude that all men will stand before the coming tribunal of God. This passage seems to refer simply to the matter of individual responsibility before God. In the end everyone must recognize that God, and not his own wisdom, or folly, or even conscience (1 Cor. 4:4), is the judge. There is nothing in this passage that would hint at a judgment other than the general judgment of all men which the New Testament speaks. In 2 Corinthians 5:10, Paul states that every individual must appear before the judgment seat of Christ so that each one shall receive that for what his life has been. Death brings the Christian nearer the day when, in company with the rest of mankind, he will have to submit to the scrutiny of divine judgment. This passage speaks only of the certainty of divine judgment and the giving of rewards or punishment. There is nothing in the passage to suggest anything other than the general concept of judgment found in the New Testament.

The great white throne judgment (Rev. 20:11–15) is one that speaks of sovereign and holy justice. In verse 12 John spoke of the dead, "great and small," standing before the throne. This passage emphasizes that all will be raised for judgment, whatever their mode of death and wherever their grave. Verses 12 and 13 indicate that all are present, not just some special class of people. This judgment scene pictures the judgment each man must receive. It is to be based on the records of two books (Rev. 20:12). The vision before us is to warn man of the fact and terror of judgment and to assure him that the terror is erased for the man whose name is in the book of life—the man redeemed by the blood of Christ. The outcome is clear. In the end men will either find their place with God or be separated from God.

In summary, it may be noted that these three judgment scenes all point toward one judgment at the last day. All men will be present. Judgment is based on what one's total life has been, including his relationship or lack of relationship to Christ. The outcome of this judgment will be an eternal destiny of blessedness in the presence of the Lord for the righteous; for the unrighteous it is destiny of eternal punishment banished from the presence of God.

In the Gospels, God is seen as the agent of judgment (Luke 12:5; John 3:36; Matt. 22:1-14). The general epistles continue this same emphasis (James 5:1-6; 1 Peter 1:17; 2:23; 4:5; 2 Peter 2:4-22; Heb. 10:30-31; 12:23). Paul, too, spoke of God as the agent in judgment (1 Thess. 4:6; 2 Thess. 1:5-6; Rom. 1:18; 9:22; 12:19; 14:10-12). However, other passages speak of Christ as the agent of judgment (John 9:39; Matt. 3:11-12; Luke 3:15-17; Matt. 19:28; Luke 22:30; John 5:22, 27; Matt. 25:31; et al.). These passages indicate that God-in-Christ is the world's Redeemer, and God-in-Christ is the world's Judge. He and he only is the Judge.

The New Testament indicates that the time of judgment will be at the resurrection (Matt. 12:41-42; Luke 11:29-32; 2 Tim. 1:12-18; 4:8; John 5:29). The major emphasis on the time of judgment is that it will be at Jesus' second coming (2 Peter 3:7, 10; 1 Thess. 5:3; 2 Thess. 1:8; 2 Tim. 4:1; Matt. 25:31-46). It appears that the New Testament sees man and his world moving toward the day which will mean the return of the Lord, the resurrection of the dead, and the final judgment upon men.

The New Testament is clear that all men will ultimately be judged by God. According to Romans 3:19, the whole world is accountable to God. Paul believes that all men will give an account to God (Rom. 14:10-12). All men, both righteous and unrighteous, will be judged by God (Acts 10:42; 2 Tim. 4:1; 1 Peter 4:5). Those who belong to Christ have nothing to fear while those who have rejected Christ will suffer the eternal consequences. The eschatological day of judgment will see a person judged according to the attitude he has taken toward Jesus in this present life. It is the same Jesus, with whom each person has to establish a relationship in the present, before whom he will have to justify himself in the future.

One idea which stands out is that throughout the New Testament where the concept of judgment is concerned is the fact that judgment—condemnation—will be related to one's total life or works. This has been observed in the three major pictures of judgment previously discussed (Matt. 25:31-46; 2 Cor. 5:10 and Rom. 14:10; Rev. 20:11-15). Another New Testament basis for judgment is unbelief (Matt. 12:38–42; 11:20–24; Luke 10:10–16; Matt. 22:1–14). This becomes clear in John's Gospel (John 3:16, 36; 12:48). This concept of unbelief in Christ as a basis of judgment is expressed clearly in 1 John 2:23. We find this concept expressed in Revelation 21:8 where the fate of unbelievers is tragically portrayed.

Sin, regarded as the breaking of the law of God, is a serious matter. But when one turns away from the gift God offers in Christ's redeeming love, that is infinitely worse. The sin of rejecting God's love in Jesus Christ is the most outrageous of all sins. In the last analysis the supreme basis of God's condemnation of persons is their relationship to Christ.

For the righteous the outcome of judgment is blessedness with God. For the unrighteous the outcome of judgment means the very opposite.

> The greatest reward of God is to bestow glory, honor, and immortality (Rom. 2:7, 10), whereas one of the most severe of the final judgments is to be excluded from the glory of God (II Thess. 1:9).[1]

CHAPTER 10

Eternal Destiny

In this chapter we will deal with the final state of those who have appeared before the judgment seat of God. The traditional view is that there is a final state which will be one of either eternal misery or eternal happiness. All who are in Christ will enjoy everlasting blessedness on the new earth, whereas all who are not in Christ will be consigned to everlasting punishment.

The doctrine of eternal punishment has been taught in the Christian church from its beginning. In the book, *The Doctrine of Eternal Punishment,* the author Harry Buis quotes a number of early Christian teachers to show that this doctrine was held by many people. He also indicates that a number of Bible scholars both of the Middle Ages and of the Reformation period taught the everlasting punishment of the wicked. Then, about the beginning of the eighteenth century, a number of Christian theologians began to deny the doctrine of eternal punishment. This denial against the doctrine "swelled into a mighty revolt in the nineteenth century, a revolt which continues to the present day."[1]

Today, the denial of the doctrine of eternal punishment usually takes the form of universalism. Universalism is the doctrine that teaches that all persons are God's children and that he will not rest until he has saved them all. Those who teach this doctrine believe that hell and eternal punishment are inconsistent with the concept of a loving and powerful God. They speak of God's justice only in terms of love. Many universalists base their scriptural arguments on at least three points: (1) The purpose of God is the restoration of things to their original excellence (Acts 3:21); (2) The means of this restoration is through Christ (Rom. 5:8; Heb. 2:9); (3) The nature of this restoration is the union of every soul with God (1 Cor. 15:24–28).

One representative of universalism is the biblical scholar, John A. T. Robinson. He rejects the concept of hell and eternal punishment on the basis of his understanding of New Testament teaching which states that every person is in Christ. He writes:

> As far as the final issue of God's purpose is concerned, there can be only one outcome. All things must be summed up in Christ, because in principle all things already are. Hell is an ultimate impossibility, because *already* there *is* no one outside Christ.[2]

We can understand the difficulties that some have with this doctrine of eternal punishment. We all naturally shrink for even thinking about such a horrible destiny. But we cannot escape the fact that the Bible speaks of eternal punishment and whether we like it or not, we must let Scripture speak to us. Let us now look at the Scripture evidence for this doctrine.

In the New Testament the word "eternal" is used to describe the destiny of both the righteous and the unrighteous. The classic example of this usage is Jesus' statement in Matthew 25:46; "And they will go away into eternal punishment, but the righteous into eternal life." These are solemn words. Each man will reap the result of his deeds and in this sense each person determines his own destiny. For one it is eternal life, for another eternal punishment.

The word "*aionios*" translated eternal has the meaning "without beginning or end." It must also be noted that eternal life refers to the quality of life as well as to the duration of life. The one who comes to Christ by faith certainly experiences a quality of life which even in this world transcends his previous life, to say nothing of what his nature will be beyond death. Jesus seemed to express this idea at times (John 4:14; 6:50-58; 8:51-52; 10:28; 11:26). However, in granting this concept, the fact that *aionios* carried the idea of duration must not be left out.

In the New Testament the word *aionios* seems to present the concept of duration. In Romans 16:26 the word is used to describe God, who is without beginning or end. In Romans 16:25 it is used of time without beginning. In many instances *aionios* is used in the New Testament to refer to that which is without end, that which is never to cease, that which is everlasting. It is used in this sense in such passages as Luke 16:9; Hebrews 5:9; 9:15; 2 Peter 1:11; 2 Timothy 2:10, as well as in many instances when Jesus used the adjective to modify life. This word is used in the same way to qualify the destiny of the unrighteous in such passages as Hebrews 6:2; 2 Thessalonians 1:9; Matthew 25:41, 46, and many others. Thus it seems that whatever qualitative sense is involved in the New Testament use of the word "eternal" the sense of duration is retained.

The Destiny of the Unrighteous

It is a biblical truth that God's love goes out to all people, that his salvation is intended for all, but that not all persons will accept God's offer of salvation in Jesus Christ. God's grace and love remain firm toward man's sins, for love cannot tolerate sin even though it encircles the sinner. Paradoxically, it is not because God's love is limited but because it is unlimited that hell is made necessary. God's wrath is not only a reaction of his holiness to sin but also a demonstration of his love which punishes for the sake of the sinner. For those who reject and deny their Lord and Savior, God's love will be destructive and chastening.

Much of what will be said has already been anticipated in the discussion of the experience of the unrighteous in the intermediate state immediately beyond death. The ideas presented here are descriptive of the eternal state of the unrighteous when the judgment of God has been carried out.

The unrighteous are to be separated from God. In Matthew 7:23; 25:41-46; and Luke 13:27; the command, "Depart from me," is used by Christ. In Matthew 25:46 there is the indication that the unrighteous will go away into eternal punishment. The phrases, "depart from me" and "go away" suggest separation from the Lord's presence. In Luke 16:25-26 there is pictured a great gulf between the rich man and Abraham. The rich man is separated from the blessings that come to the beggar Lazarus. In Revelation 21:8, 27 and 22:15 we have a picture of the unrighteous shut off from the eternal city in which the righteous enjoy the presence and fellowship of Christ.

The unrighteous are to have their eternal dwelling place in hell. The word "*gehenna*," translated hell, has the meaning of the place of punishment in the next life. Gehenna is a transliteration of the Hebrew term *Ge Hinnom*, that is, the Valley of Hinnom. The Valley of Hinnom was located southeast of the city of Jerusalem. In ancient times it had been the location of the worship of the heathen god, Molech, which included burning babies alive. This practice was abolished by King Josiah (2 Kings 23:10), and the place became a refuse dump, including the disposal of bodies of animals, and the bodies of criminals who had no one to give them burial. A fire was kept going continuously for sanitary purposes. The final insult offered to an executed criminal was that his body was cast into Gehenna (Matt. 5:22). Thus it became symbolic of the final spiritual state of the unrighteous in Matthew 10:28 and Mark 9:43.

Apart from occurring in James 3:6 (where the word Gehenna is used to refer to an undisciplined tongue set on fire by hell), this word was used only by Jesus. In Matthew 5:29-30, Jesus uses this term implying Gehenna as a place of judgment for the unrighteous. The same emphasis appears in Matthew 10:28 and Luke 12:5. The language of Mark 9:43-48 is most dramatic. The picture of destruction is to be understood as picture language. It should neither be explained away nor understood apart from the whole record of Jesus' person, work, and words.

These passages indicate that Jesus used the word Gehenna to describe the place of the wicked in terms which spoke of horror and abomination. This hell of fire was a place originally prepared for the devil and his angels (Matt. 25:41) but now becomes a place of punishment for the wicked. In their rebellion against God and the rejection of his love in Jesus Christ, they have turned to Satan and become like him. They have chosen their place and their destiny.

> There are only two kinds of people in the end, those who say to God, "Thy will be done," and those to whom God says, in the end, "Thy will be done." All that are in Hell, choose it. Without that self-choice there could be no Hell.[3]

What is the nature of the unbeliever's life and existence? Paul spoke of death as the wages of sin (Rom. 6:23). This death is wages for work done in contrast to the gift of eternal life that could never be earned. "Death" as a descriptive term for the destiny of the wicked is graphically presented in Revelation 20:10–11 and 20:6, 14. In these passages the destiny of the wicked is termed "the second death." The unbeliever dies and finds another "death" awaiting him.

In some passages in the New Testament, the destiny of the wicked is described as "destruction" (2 Thess. 1:9; Phil. 3:17–19). Other times the eternal destiny of the wicked is spoken of in terms of punishment (Heb. 10:30–31; Matt. 25:46). Other passages speak of the eternal destiny of the wicked in terms of darkness (Matt. 25:30; 22:13; 2 Peter 2:17; Jude 13). Finally, there are those passages which describe the destiny of the wicked in terms of fire (Luke 16:19–31; Matt. 18:8–9; Mark 9:43–48; Rev. 20:14–15; 21:8).

To deny the biblical doctrine of hell is to fail to be realistic; it is to be ignorant of the depths of sin into which many in the human race have fallen. The overall biblical witness indicates that there is a moral strictness about the love of God which cannot be presumed upon.

Men and women appear before God in the robe of the character woven here on earth. Those who hate God here will hate Him there; the morally careless in daily life will be morally careless still; the defiant will continue defiant, and the unclean will remain uncleansed and unrepentant.[4]

Men sentence themselves in their choice of living without God. God's judgment then simply becomes divine approval of man's choice. God will not have men's enforced obedience. One of the persistent traditions, expressed by some Christian theologians over the centuries is that God gave men to choose whether or not they wish to enter into a relationship with him. If man chooses against God, God does not cease to respect his freedom. Other Christian thinkers (Augustine, Aquinas, Luther, and Calvin) emphasized the sovereign power of God. The biblical witness affirms both the sovereign power of God in human destiny and the freedom of the will. Man may reject the goodness of God and prefer evil, reject eternal life and prefer death. And God, who created man, who loves man, will not make man say "yes." Indeed, according to the Bible, God may take man's "no" for an answer.

We can affirm salvation on the other side of death for those who are in Christ since this has scriptural support, but we cannot preach that any of those banished to hell will finally be saved. We believe in a loving and sovereign God whose love and sovereignity extend throughout eternity. Therefore, in a sense we can be assured that those in hell are in the hands of a God who is both merciful and righteous, and that we can trust God that his mercy as well as his justice will be manifest among them. While this legitimate pastoral concern is warranted by biblical teaching, the doctrine of a final universal salvation is not clearly taught by the scriptural witness.

The Biblical ideas about eternal punishment and hell add a note of moral seriousness to our beliefs. We must struggle with this seriousness and attempt to understand it. We must speak about hell, but we do it with reluctance, with grief, and some tears—but speak about it we must. It is an undeniable part of the biblical record and it provides a significant urgency for the Christian's pastoral and missionary zeal. For our missionary enterprise, the doctrine of hell should spur us on to greater zeal and urgency. Our message must never deny the Gospel truth, "For God so loved the world that he gave his only Son, that whoever believes in him should not perish but have eternal life" (John 3:16).

The Destiny of the Righteous

The New Testament speaks of heaven as the eternal destiny of the righteous. Heaven represents a sphere of existence about which we have no firsthand knowledge and therefore we can only talk about it in symbolic language. We can catch glimpses of its splendor, but its full glory is beyond our present comprehension.

Heaven is the abode of the righteous. In contrast to the wicked, the righteous are spoken of as being in fellowship with God, or in a relationship of blessedness and fellowship with God. This seems to be the implication of Jesus' words when he spoke of Lazarus as being in "Abraham's bosom" (Luke 16: 19-31). The same emphasis appears in Jesus' words, "Enter into the joy of your master" (Matt. 25:21), and "Come, O blessed of my Father, inherit the kingdom prepared for you from the foundation of the world" (Matt. 25:34). The relationship of blessedness and fellowship with God is represented in Jesus' statement, "Father, I desire that they also, whom thou hast given me, may be with me where I am" (John 17:24). This prayer of Jesus looks forward to the time when believers will be with Christ in God.

Paul saw the destiny of the believers as being with the Lord (1 Thess. 4:17). He believed that when the believer departed this life, he was to be with the Lord (Phil. 1:23; 2 Cor. 5:8). These verses are sufficient to show that the righteous beyond this life shall live in a state of blessedness and fellowship with God in Jesus Christ.

The place of the abode of the righteous is spoken of as heaven. The Greek word "*ouranos,*" translated heaven, means "a part of the universe," that is, the sky, atmosphere, that which stands over the earth, or "the abode of the divine," that is, the dwelling place of God, of Christ, the angels. It is the Greek equivalent for the Hebrew *shamayim*, which means "the upper regions" or "the heights above." Man, looking up to God, pictures the place of God's dwelling and of man's dwelling with him in heaven, the heights above.

Jesus describes heaven as "my Father's house" (John 14:2). In Luke 15:7, when Jesus spoke of the joy in heaven when one sinner repents, heaven is implied as the dwelling place of God. In Hebrews 9:23-24, the author states that Jesus entered heaven to appear before the face of God in carrying out his priestly intercession. Heaven then is seen as the place of God's dwelling.

Heaven is also seen as the ultimate home of the redeemed. Heaven is pictured as a heavenly country and an abiding city (Heb. 11:13-16). Peter spoke of the believer's incorruptible inheritance in heaven (1 Peter 1:3-4). Paul understood that the Christian's relationship is in heaven (Phil. 3:20); their master is in heaven (Col. 4:1; Eph. 6:9); they have an eternal house in heaven (2 Cor. 5:1). The New Testament writers considered the ultimate home of the redeemed as being heaven.

The New Testament speaks of a believer entering into eternal life when by faith he relates himself to Christ. This means that to some degree he experiences the quality of life now that will come to the complete state in the experience of resurrection. There are many references in the New Testament that speak of this eternal life of the believer (Luke 10:25ff; 18:18; Mark 10:17, 30; Matt. 19:16; John 3:15-16; 6:27, 40, 47, 50-51; 11:25-26; Heb. 5:9; Rom. 8:10; Gal. 6:7-9; 1 Tim. 1:16; 6:12; and many others). It will be a life that will transcend this life in all that we know and experience.

The ultimate home of the redeemed is spoken of as rest (Heb. 3:11, 18; 4:1, 3, 8-9). When God completed his work of creation, he "rested"; so his people, having completed their service on earth, will enter into his rest. The same idea is found in Revelation 14:13. To obtain rest in the eternal state does not mean idleness. Heaven is not so much a place where no work is done as one where pain has ceased. On the basis of our study we believe that there will be a number of activities in heaven, e.g., worship, service, learning, fellowship, etc., which will be a continuation of our labor for Christ here on earth, without, of course, exhaustion, weariness or failure. In the eternal state, believers will come to renewed strength and refreshment after the toil of this life.

There are three pictures that describe the ultimate home of the redeemed. They appear in Revelation 21:1 to 22:5. They speak a message of comfort and assurance to the people of Christ who experience suffering, pain, loneliness, and persecution.

The first picture is of a new heaven and a new earth (Rev. 21:1-8). Paul believed that creation itself will be redeemed from the bondage of decay (Rom. 8:19-25). The author of 2 Peter interprets the change as being set free through the cleansing and purifying process of fire (3:7-13). This cleansed and restored earth will be the "new heaven and the new earth" of Revelation 21:1-8. The word translated "new" in Revelation 21:1 is "kainos." It means basically new in kind. The use of this word implies that there will be a new kind of heaven and earth which will be the dwelling place for God's people. The whole universe was created by God, therefore it had a definite beginning. The same God who created the universe will redeem it, therefore it has a definite goal. The One who created the universe is at the same time its Redeemer.

The expression in verse 1, "the sea was no more," suggests that in this new heaven and earth separation will be no more. The sea was a symbol of the many nations in ceaseless unrest, in godless antagonism, and in deep mystery of sin. It symbolized all that kept men separated from God and his fellowman. In this new heaven and earth, there will be nothing to stand between a man and God. God himself will dwell with men. He will remove every indication of the distressing experiences which are known in this life (Rev. 21:3-4). These things will not be in the new order; they belong to the old order which has ended.

John now speaks and quotes the one on the throne saying, "Behold, I make all things new" (Rev. 21:5). Salvation in the biblical sense includes the redemption of creation as well as of men. With this new creation, God's plan of creation reaches its goal. In it a redeemed humanity is transformed to the image of Jesus Christ which marks the children of God. The redemption of mankind, however, is followed by the transformation and renewal of creation, in which all the laws of the struggle for existence, of suffering and of temporal experience, no longer prevail. Indeed, all things are made new.

The second picture is of heaven as a city (Rev. 21:9-27). John sees the new city, Jerusalem, coming down from heaven. It has a great high wall surrounding it. The walled city in ancient times was for the protection of its people. The great wall symbolizes God's perfect and complete protection of his people. Ancient walled cities usually had one gate which was closed at night or when an enemy approached. This new city has twelve gates guarded by twelve angels. Entrance into God's city is not open to anyone who chooses to enter, but only to those to whom God gives the right.

The spaciousness of the city is seen in its measurement. It is in the shape of a cube, ". . . its length and breadth and height are equal" (Rev. 21:16). This shape is that of the Holy of Holies (1 Kings 6:20) and indicates perfection. The measurements are not to be regarded as literal measurements but rather represent the ideal symmetry, perfection, vastness, and completeness of the new Jerusalem. The high dimensions are for the purpose of saying that there will be room for all of God's people in the "new Jerusalem."

The beauty of the city is described in terms of gold and jewels. The twelve foundations of the city were twelve precious stones. The city itself was built of pure gold, clear as glass. The new city will reflect the glory of God, which human language cannot describe. There is no need for illuminating power in this city, which needs neither sun nor moon, "for the glory of God is its light, and its lamp is the Lamb" (Rev. 21:23). There is no temple in the new city for there is no longer any need of sacrifice and intercession. God himself dwells among his people.

> Such is the New Jerusalem, the eternal home of man and the eternal tabernacle of God. It is the glorified environment and glorified society which corresponds to the glorified soul and glorified body of the redeemed.[5]

Heaven, then, as John saw it, is a perfect city, offering for God's people an abundant entrance, perfect beauty, and perfect protection.

The third picture of heaven is described as a garden (Rev. 22:1-5). The word "garden" is not used in this passage, but everything descriptive of a garden is there. In this garden a "river of the water of life" has its source in the throne of God and the Lamb. Life takes its origin from God for the river flowed from the throne of God. On either side of the river grows the tree of life bearing its fruit continually. Its leaves have healing powers. That which is necessary to sustain life, water, food, and health is provided. In powerful symbolism, John is saying that God has the ability to provide all that is needed for eternal life.

There will be no curse, no handicaps in heaven. God's people will see him and serve him forever. The Garden of Eden meant that God has made man to have communion with him in a perfect environment. True human life is essentially life in such a perfect environment. Therefore the perfection of the Christian life involves the perfection of the earth as well as heaven. The Christian life is fulfilled only in a new heaven and a new earth filled with transformed people living in holy loving fellowship with God and with one another, in harmony with a transformed and renewed creation (Isa. 11:6-9; 65:17-25).

For the righteous, heaven is a place of perfect fellowship, perfect protection, perfect provision of needs, and perfect service to God. God and man will be dwelling together, a relationship never to be interrupted. At last we shall behold the face of Jesus Christ and we shall be like him as we see him as he is.

"Maranatha!"

"Come, Lord Jesus!"

CHAPTER 11

A Last Word

Our study of biblical eschatology was undertaken for three reasons: to provide the Christian with a view of history and the assurance of its final consummation, to assure the Christian of his ultimate destiny, and to correct a wrong emphasis in eschatology.

Every Christian has a right to his convictions about biblical truth, but since we "have this treasure in earthen vessels" none of us are infallible. There will be many who will find this study of biblical eschatology helpful to their own thinking. Those who are dispensational or premillennial in their thinking will have to recognize that there is another viewpoint of biblical eschatology that is biblically valid. No one has the right to think or act as if he or she were the sole possessor of truth. No one will advance his position by attacking someone who holds an opposite view.

In developing this understanding of biblical eschatology I have tried to be fair in presenting contrasting positions. Where I have differed with a particular interpretation I have sought to justify our position biblically and theologically, and not by questioning one's integrity or Christian witness. While it is fair to attempt to prove a position illogical, it is unjustifiable to belittle someone who holds an opposite viewpoint.

Biblical eschatology is in harmony with dispensational and premillennial brethren on some of the important doctrines of the Christian faith: the doctrine of the divine inspiration of Holy Scripture, the virgin birth and deity of Jesus Christ, the bodily resurrection of Jesus Christ from the dead, the substitutionary atonement, eternal salvation by grace through faith in Christ, the importance of godly living, and hope for the future in the bodily return of Jesus Christ. Those who differ on some doctrines may remember that there are those areas in which they are united. It is not our intention to make a system of biblical eschatology the criteria for Christian fellowship. With the apostle Paul we affirm that "there is one body and one Spirit, . . . one Lord, one faith, one baptism, one God and Father of us all, who is above all and through all and in all" (Eph. 4:4–6).

I believe that we have developed a guide to a balanced view of eschatology that can function in several ways. First, it can provide an individual or a discussion group with a general introduction to biblical eschatology. Second, it can be used as resource material for the church school teacher or pastor who is teaching eschatology in a classroom situation. Third, it provides an alternative to the one-sided eschatological position presented in many popular books and films. And finally, for the believer who is confused or unsure of what the Bible says about life in the present and in the future, this guide can be helpful in allowing him to discover the biblical teaching concerning his eternal destiny.

The undertaking of this study has been prompted by the desire to encourage and strengthen the believer in his faith by providing him with an understanding of biblical eschatology. It is our hope that this has been accomplished.

RESOURCES FOR STUDY

A Word to Teachers

I am a great believer in small group Bible studies. Participation in these studies has done more to make the Bible come alive, to stimulate growth in Christians, and to lead others to Christ, than any other method I know. Bible study has been spiritually productive in my own life.

I have known the fear of leading a Bible study. Much of my fear was the result of a mistaken idea I held. That idea was that I could not lead a Bible study unless I had all the answers, and since I did not have all the answers, I became frightened of hard questions. I soon learned that one could lead a Bible study and not have to be the "expert," the one with all the answers. A genuine concern for people, a spirit of openness and love, and a desire to learn what the Bible has to say about life, is all that is necessary for a person to be a Bible study teacher. I have yet to find a person who has these basic attributes who has not become a good Bible study teacher.

The following principles will help in leading a Bible study group.

(1) Each member of the group should have a copy of the book and study guide. A good translation of the Bible, rather than a paraphrase, is important since translations tend to be more faithful to the Hebrew and Greek. I prefer the New International Version or the Revised Standard Version for my personal study (however, there are other good translations available.)

(2) The Bible study group should have access to Bible commentaries, Bible dictionaries, and Bible concordances. Those persons who enjoy serious Bible study should invest some money in a good Bible commentary, dictionary, and concordance. Several are listed in the book list.

(3) The leader of a study should be familiar with material under study so that he/she can guide the discussion along and keep the study on target. Remember, the leader does not have to have all the answers. The answers are discovered by the group as they study the text. What is personally discovered is always more one's own than something that is taught in a lecture form.

(4) The leader should be careful not to talk too much. Allow time for group discussion. If you wait, others will speak up and share their thoughts. When the leader rushes from question to question, people become rigid and mechanical. What develops then is not a discussion group but a kind of question and answer game where little is remembered. And, if someone is always quick to give an answer, invite others of the group to respond by asking, "What do the rest of you think?" or, "Does someone have another thought on this?"

(5) Finally, but certainly not the least important, pray that God will make the group congenial and open minded, and that he will be the real teacher as you discuss the Bible together.

The following materials provide additional helps for those who will be teaching Bible study groups or Sunday school classes: *Leading Bible Discussions* by James F. Nyquist (Downers Grove: Intervarsity Press, 1967); *Teach Me to Teach* by Dorothy G. Swain (Valley Forge: Judson Press, 1964); and *All About Bible Study* by Herbert Lockyer (Grand Rapids: Zondervan Publishing House, 1977). The books by Nyquist or Lockyer suggest and discuss methods and techniques of Bible study in groups. The book by Swain discusses the role of the teacher in a Bible study or Sunday school class. Many other materials are available from denominational publishers that can be used in guiding persons with leading Bible study or Sunday school classes.

Study Questions

Chapter 1: The Meaning and Necessity of Eschatology

FOR REFLECTION AND DISCUSSION

1. If you were teaching a church school class and someone asked you to define eschatology, what would you say?

2. Several subjects are covered in any discussion of eschatology. What subjects do you think are most important? least important? Why?

3. In your own words briefly state the three reasons given for the necessity of a biblical eschatology. If you were asked to state two other reasons, what would you suggest?

4. Is there any relation between an understanding of eschatology and the work of Christian missions? If so, what would it be? (See Acts 17:30–31; 2 Cor. 5:20–21; Matt. 28:16–20.)

5. In your own words, how would you define apocalyptic?

6. The church school teacher asks you to present a four-minute summary of how apocalyptic literature differs from other kinds of literature. You agree to this and now the time for your report has arrived. What would you say?

7. In your own words what would you say is the purpose of the apocalyptist's message?

FOR FURTHER REFLECTION

1. List several examples of non-Christian eschatology. How do they compare with your understanding of biblical eschatology?

2. Do you see any relationship between eschatology and a "Christian lifestyle?" Give reasons for your answer.

3. Do you think that ministers preach too many or too few sermons on subjects relating to eschatology? Give reasons for your opinion.

4. In your opinion do you see any danger in laying too much stress on the future? on past experiences and present circumstances? If so what is the danger and how can it be avoided?

5. Can you suggest several present-day situations that have taken on the apocalyptic character?

6. In your opinion, do you see any relevance in apocalyptic in today's world?

Chapter 2: Types of Eschatology

FOR REFLECTION AND DISCUSSION

1. What are the distinctive features of consistent eschatology? realized eschatology? idealized eschatology? dispensational eschatology? systematic eschatology? What are the strengths and weaknesses of each view? How does each view compare with inaugurated eschatology? (If you are in a study group, you might want to divide into groups of two or three and each group take a view to report on.)

2. Basic to inaugurated eschatology is the concept of the "kingdom of God." In your own words, what does "kingdom of God" mean to you?

3. C. H. Dodd, who coined the phrase "realized eschatology," believes there will be no further eschatological events. Would you agree or disagree with him? Why? Would you agree with his interpretation of the second coming of Jesus? Why or why not?

4. Which one of the six types of eschatology is closest to your church background? Which type do you think is closest to your understanding of biblical eschatology?

FOR FURTHER REFLECTION

1. Do you agree with Albert Schweitzer's view of Jesus? Support your answer from your own understanding of what you know about Jesus.

2. From your understanding of realized eschatology, briefly state how it differs from consistent eschatology.

3. In dispensational eschatology the method of interpreting Scripture has been called "consistent literalism." First, what is your understanding of consistent literalism? Second, do you agree with this method of interpretation? Give reasons for your answer.

4. Would you agree with the dispensational interpretation of the millennium? the rapture? Give reasons for your answer.

5. Is dispensational eschatology faithful to the gospel of Jesus Christ? State reasons for your answer.

6. "In the life, death, and resurrection of Jesus the new age was inaugurated. In a real sense the future has become the present, salvation is realized, and Christians can enjoy God's kingdom." Based on your understanding of inaugurated eschatology, how would you communicate this statement to a person who does not claim to be Christian?

Chapter 3: Biblical Understanding of Eschatology

FOR REFLECTION AND DISCUSSION

1. In your own words, what do you understand to be the one great task assigned to the church? (See Matt. 24:14 or Mark 13:10.) What are some of the ways in which this task can be carried out?

2. The author states that "inaugurated eschatology best describes the eschatology of the New Testament." Do you agree or disagree with this statement? State reasons for your answer.

3. In your own words, describe "salvation."

4. If you were asked to give a three-minute report on why you believe biblical eschatology completes God's redemptive process what would you say?

FOR FURTHER REFLECTION

1. "We have the New Testament with the teaching of Jesus, therefore the Old Testament, apart from the Psalms, is of little value to us." How would you respond to this statement in light of biblical eschatology's concern with history?

2. Would it be possible to develop a biblical eschatology apart from the life and work of Jesus Christ? Give reasons for your answer.

3. Do you think it is necessary to have an understanding of biblical eschatology? State several reasons for your position.

Chapter 4: Death

FOR REFLECTION AND DISCUSSION

1. How would you describe "travelog eschatology"? Do you think it is necessary to establish one? State your reasons.

2. If you were asked by someone to briefly state what the Old Testament has to say about death, what would you say?

3. Read and discuss the following Scripture passages as they relate to the hope of life after death:
   a. Isaiah 26:10-14   c. Daniel 12:2
   b. Isaiah 26:16-19

4. What do you understand to be the relationship between sin and death? (See Romans 6:16, 20-21, 23.) What do you think Paul means by "death" in Romans 6:23?

FOR FURTHER REFLECTION

1. How would you describe the Old Testament view of life after death in Sheol? Compare this existence of life after death in Sheol to life before death.

2. What do you think Jesus meant when he used the metaphor of "sleeping" referring to death? Share your feelings about your understanding of death.

3. What do you understand the gospel to say about death? What biblical reference can you suggest that speaks to this question?

4. Does biblical teaching on death help you in facing your own death? How? Explain your responses as best you can.

Chapter 5: The Intermediate State

FOR REFLECTION AND DISCUSSION

1. What is your understanding of the concept of purgatory?

2. If you were to define or explain "paradise" what would you say? Give reasons for your answer.

FOR FURTHER REFLECTION

1. In your own words, describe the state of the righteous after death. Compare this with what the text has to say about the state of the unrighteous.

2. Is there a difference between Old Testament "Sheol" and the intermediate state in the New Testament?

3. Many Protestants reject the concept of purgatory. On what basis do you think this rejection is made?

Chapter 6: The Second Coming of Jesus

FOR REFLECTION AND DISCUSSION

1. Read and discuss the following passages concerning the second coming of Jesus answering two questions: First, what does the passage say? And second, what does this passage mean to me?

a. Luke 17:22-37
b. 2 Peter 3:1-10
c. Acts 1:11

d. Matthew 24:25—29:30
e. 1 Thessalonians 4:13-18

2. In your own words state the meaning of Jesus' words in Mark 13:32 or Matthew 24:36.

3. Do you agree or disagree with the following statement: "The signs relating to Jesus' return cannot be used to calculate the future, rather they are intended to be a summons to watchfulness for the coming of the Lord, a perseverance in the faith, and missionary service in the Lord." State reasons for your answer.

4. What is your understanding of the term "rapture"? When do you think it will occur?

FOR FURTHER REFLECTION

1. Hebrews 9:28 mentions two comings of Christ. In your own words, state the meaning of this verse.

2. You are asked to give a brief exposition of Acts 1:7-8. What would you say?

3. Read Acts 2:1-36. How would you respond to the statement, "We are living in the last days?" (See Hebrews 1:1-2.)

4. In your own words compare Paul's view of the antichrist with John's view of the antichrist. What is your understanding of the antichrist?

Chapter 7: The Millennium

FOR REFLECTION AND DISCUSSION

1. As the group leader in a Bible study, you have been asked to comment on the millennium. In your own words, what is the millennium and what are the three major views of the millennium?

2. Ask several people to assume one of the following positions and defend its particular view of the millennium.
a. premillennial
b. postmillennial

c. dispensational
d. amillennial

3. Would you agree with the following statement: The millennium represents the "period of time between the two advents of our Lord, that is, as going on at the present time and ending when our Lord returns."

FOR FURTHER REFLECTION

1. Does the view of the millennium in question 3 above differ from the author's position? If so, how does it differ? If not, why?

2. In your own words state the author's view of the millennium. Do you agree with this view? Give reasons for your answer.

3. Now state your position of the millennium. Give reasons to support your answer.

Chapter 8: The Resurrection

FOR REFLECTION AND DISCUSSION

1. What do you understand to be the difference between resuscitation and resurrection? Cite examples of each.

2. Do you agree or disagree with the following statement: "Remove the reality of the resurrection of Christ and you destroy the Christian faith." Read and discuss Paul's argument in 1 Corinthians 15:12-19.

3. What do you understand to be the ultimate hope promised to the righteous? Cite several biblical references you would use to support your position.

FOR FURTHER REFLECTION

1. What would be your understanding of Paul's comments in Philippians 3:21?

2. From your understanding, how would you describe the nature of the believer's resurrection body? What would you say is the purpose of the resurrection body?

3. "When Jesus returns only the righteous will be raised. The unrighteous will be raised after the millennium." Do you agree or disagree with this statement? Give reasons for your answer.

Chapter 9: The Judgment

FOR REFLECTION AND DISCUSSION

1. Do you believe in an ultimate judgment by God? Give reasons why you believe as you do.

2. The author indicates that the three judgment scenes (Matt. 25:31-46; Rom. 14:10 and 2 Cor. 5:10; Rev. 20:11-15) speak only of one judgment at the last day. What is your understanding of these scenes? Give reasons for your positions.

FOR FURTHER REFLECTION

1. John 5:24 states believers will "not come into judgment." How would you explain this verse?

2. Will the sinful deeds of Christians be revealed in the final judgment?
   a. If you answer *YES*, will that not make the final judgment a terrible ordeal even for believers?
   b. If you answer *NO*, how would you explain the following passages:
      (1) Ecclesiastes 12:14
      (2) Matthew 12:36
      (3) Romans 2:16
      (4) 1 Corinthians 4:5

Chapter 10: Eternal Destiny

FOR REFLECTION AND DISCUSSION

1. Do you believe in a hell? Give reasons to support your answer.

2. If you were asked to describe heaven, what would you say?

3. How would you describe paradise?

4. Read John 14:2-3.
   a. How would you explain verse 2?
   b. What does verse 3 mean to you?

5. Do you believe that this earth will be part of a "new heaven and new earth"? Give reasons for your answer.

FOR FURTHER REFLECTION

1. How would you explain the "second death"?

2. Read 2 Peter 3:8-13.
   a. Does verse 10 prove that the universe will be destroyed by a nuclear bomb? Give reasons for your answer.
   b. Does the passage harmonize or clash with the idea of evolution? State your reason.

3. Are heaven and hell places where people will spend eternity, or are they states of existence that can be present now as well as in the future? Are there other possible explanations or meanings that can be given to these terms.

4. If you were the Evangelist John writing today, what pictures would you use to describe heaven?

Notes

Chapter 1. The Meaning and Necessity of Eschatology

1. Charles F. Pfeiffer, *Between the Testaments* (Grand Rapids: Baker Book House, 1959), p. 81.
2. D. S. Russell, *The Method and Message of Jewish Apocalyptic*, Old Testament Library (Philadelphia: Westminster Press, 1964), pp. 104—139.
3. Leon Morris, *Apocalyptic* (Grand Rapids: Wm. B. Eerdmans Publishing Co., 1972), p. 36.
4. George E. Ladd, "Apocalyptic," *The New Bible Dictionary*, eds. J. D. Douglas et al. (Grand Rapids: Wm. B. Eerdmans Publishing Co., 1962), p. 43.
5. George E. Ladd, "Apocalyptic, Apocalypse," *Baker's Dictionary of Theology*, eds. Everett F. Harrison, Geoffrey W. Bromiley, and Carl F. H. Henry (Grand Rapids: Baker Book House, 1960), pp. 52—53.

Chapter 2. Types of Eschatology

1. R. H. Fuller, *The Mission and Achievement of Jesus*, Studies in Biblical Theology, No. 12 (Chicago: Alec R. Allenson, 1954), p. 116.
2. George R. Beasley-Murray, *A Commentary on Mark Thirteen* (London: Macmillan & Co., 1957), p. 87.
3. Albert Schweitzer, *The Quest for the Historical Jesus*, trans. W. Montgomery (New York: Macmillan, 1948), pp. 370—371.
4. C. H. Dodd, *The Parables of the Kingdom*, rev. ed. (New York: Scribners, 1961), p. 35.
5. C. H. Dodd, *The Apostolic Preaching and Its Developments* (New York: Harper & Bros., 1960), p. 94.
6. Paul Althaus, "Eschatology," *A Handbook of Christian Theology*, eds. Marvin Halverson and Arthur A. Cohen (New York: Meridian Books, 1958), pp. 103—104.
7. Charles Caldwell Ryrie, *Dispensationalism Today* (Chicago: Moody Press, 1965), p. 31.

8. *Ibid.*, pp. 57—64.
9. *Ibid.*, p. 97.
10. Charles L. Feinberg, *Premillennialism or Amillennialism*, second and enlarged ed. (Wheaton: Van Kampen Press, Inc., 1954), p. 197.
11. Ryrie, p. 158.
12. John F. Walvoord, *The Return of the Lord* (Grand Rapids: Zondervan Publishing House, 1955), p. 34.
13. *Ibid.*, p. 54.
14. Clarence B. Bass, *Backgrounds to Dispensationalism* (Grand Rapids: Wm. B. Eerdmans Publishing co., 1960), p. 149.
15. Augustus H. Strong, *Systematic Theology*, Vol. III (Philadelphia: The Griffith and Rowland Press, 1909), p. 997.

Chapter 3. Biblical Understanding of Eschatology
1. George E. Ladd, *The Presence of the Future* (Grand Rapids: Wm. B. Eerdmans Publishing Co., 1974), p. 144.

Chapter 4. Death
1. Page H. Kelly, *Broadman Bible Commentary*, Vol. 5, eds. Clifton J. Allen, et al. (Nashville: Broadman Press, 1971), p. 267; and D. S. Russell, p. 368.
2. Edward J. Young, "Daniel," *The New Bible Commentary*, rev. eds. Donald Guthrie et al. (Grand Rapids: Wm. B. Eerdmans Publishing Co., 1970), p. 702.
3. Dale Moody, *The Hope of Glory* (Grand Rapids: Wm. B. Eerdmans Publishing Co., 1964), pp. 55—56.
4. Bernard Ramm, *Them He Glorified* (Grand Rapids: Wm. B. Eerdmans Publishing Co., 1963), p. 83.
5. C. S. Lewis, *Miracles* (New York: The Macmillan Co., 1947), p. 151.
6. Leon Morris, *The Wages of Sin* (London: The Tyndale Press, 1954), p. 28.

Chapter 5. The Intermediate State
1. Walter Kunneth, *The Theology of the Resurrection*, trans. James W. Leitch (St. Louis: Concordia Publishing House, 1965), p. 274.
2. *Ibid.*, p. 275.
3. Richard P. McBrien, *Catholicism*, Vol. II (Minneapolis, Winston Press, 1980), p. 1144.
4. John E. Steinmueller and Kathryn Sullivan, *Catholic Encyclopedia: New Testament* (New York: Joseph F. Wagner, Inc., 1950), p. 534.

5. Joseph Pohle, *Eschatology or the Catholic Doctrine of the Last Things*, ed. Arthur Preuss (St. Louis: B. Herder Book Co., 1917), p. 80.
6. Steinmueller and Sullivan, p. 534.
7. Elmar Klinger, "Purgatory," *Sacramentum Mundi*, eds. Karl Rahner, et al., Vol V (New York: Herder and Herder, 1970), p. 168.

Chapter 6. The Second Coming of Jesus

1. Harold A. Guy, *The New Testament Doctrine of 'Last Things'* (London: Oxford University Press, 1948), pp. 77—78.
2. John A. T. Robinson, *In the End, God. . .* (London, James Clark & Co., Ltd., 1950), p. 66.
3. Guy, p. 181.
4. George E. Ladd, *The Blessed Hope* (Grand Rapids: Wm. B. Eerdmans Publishing Co., 1956), p. 6.
5. G. C. Berkouwer, *The Return of Christ*, trans. James Van Oosterom (Grand Rapids: Wm. B. Eerdmans Publishing Co., 1972), p. 155.
6. Emil Brunner, *Eternal Hope*, trans. Harold Knight (London: Lutterworth Press, 1954), pp. 138—139.
7. Oscar Cullman, *The Early Church*, ed. and trans. A. J. B. Higgins (Philadelphia: Westminster Press, 1956), p. 158.
8. Leon J. Wood, *The Bible and Future Events* (Grand Rapids: Zondervan Publishing House, 1973), p. 76.
9. *Ibid.*, p. 42.
10. Walvoord, p. 82.
11. J. Barton Payne, *The Imminent Appearing of Christ* (Grand Rapids: Wm. B. Eerdmans Publishing Co., 1962), p. 105.
12. Berkouwer, p. 288.

Chapter 7. The Millennium

1. Wood, p. 161.
2. C. Norman Krause, *Dispensationalism in America* (Richmond: John Knox Press, 1958), p. 132.
3. Thomas F. Torrance, *The Apocalypse Today* (London: James Clark & Co., 1960), pp. 162—163.
4. George E. Ladd, *A Commentary on the Revelation of John* (Grand Rapids: Wm. B. Eerdmans Publishing Co., 1972), p. 262.
5. Wood, p. 166.
6. Berkouwer, p. 307.

Chapter 8. The Resurrection
1. Jürgen Moltmann, *The Theology of Hope*, trans. James W. Leitch (New York: Harper & Row, 1967), p. 180.
2. Berkouwer, p. 180.
3. Ray Summers, *The Life Beyond* (Nashville: Broadman Press, 1951), p. 31.
4. J. A. Schep, *The Nature of the Resurrection Body* (Grand Rapids: Wm. B. Eerdmans Publishing Co., 1964), p. 182.
5. Wood, p. 34.
6. Walvoord, p. 43.

Chapter 9. The Judgment
1. Ramm, p. 27.

Chapter 10. Eternal Destiny
1. Harry Buis, *The Doctrine of Eternal Punishment* (Philadelphia: Presbyterian and Reformed Publishing Co., 1957), p. 111.
2. Robinson, p. 119.
3. C. S. Lewis, *The Great Divorce* (New York: The Macmillan Co., 1946), p. 72.
4. J. A. Motyer, *After Death*, Christian Foundations (Philadelphia: Westminster Press, 1966), p. 40.
5. Ramm, p. 115.

Selected Bibliography

Reference Books

Douglas, J. D. (editor). *The New Bible Dictionary.* Grand Rapids: Wm. B. Eerdmans Publishing Co., 1962.

This Bible dictionary, written by an international team of 139 scholars, discusses not only people and places, geography and history, customs and culture of Bible lands and times, but it also discusses doctrines of the Christian faith such as justification, salvation, revelation, inspiration, holiness, as well as many other teachings.

Guthrie, Donald, J. A. Motyer, A. M. Stibbs, D. J. Wiseman. *The New Bible Commentary: Revised.* 3d. rev. ed. Grand Rapids: Wm. B. Eerdmans Publishing Co., 1970.

This commentary, written by an international team of 51 scholars, covers each book of the Bible. Also included are discussions on the authority of Scripture, revelation and inspiration, the theology of the Old Testament as well as several other general subjects.

Harrison, Everett F. *Baker's Dictionary of Theology.* Grand Rapids: Baker Book House, 1960.

In this dictionary are defined biblical terms of theological significance as well as subjects of importance in the history of theology. An international list of scholars numbering 138 have contributed to this reference book. A must for serious students of the Bible.

Kelly, Balmer H., and others. *The Layman's Bible Commentary.* 25 vol. Richmond: John Knox Press, 1959-1964.

This multivolume commentary is written in non-technical language for the layman and is designed for personal Bible study.

Metzger, Bruce M., and Isobel M. Metzger (compilers). *The Oxford Concise Concordance to the Revised Standard Version of the Holy Bible.* New York: Oxford University Press, 1962.

This concordance is intended to meet the needs of the general reader of the Bible. This concordance is keyed to the RSV and is a good small selective concordance.

Young, Robert. *Young's Analytical Concordance to the Bible.* Rev. ed. Grand Rapids: Wm. B. Eerdmans Publishing Co., 1955.

This massive concordance lists more than 311,000 references in English subdivided under the Hebrew and Greek originals. This concordance is keyed to the KJV of the Bible, nevertheless it still remains a valuable reference book.

Books for lay persons

Adams, Jay. *The Time Is at Hand.* Philadelphia: Presbyterian Reformed Publishing Co., 1970.

The author discusses several themes of eschatology from what he calls a "realized millennialism." He interacts with those who hold different viewpoints.

Armerding, Carl E., and W. Ward Gasque, eds. *Dreams, Visions, & Oracles.* Grand Rapids: Baker Book House, 1976.

This book, designed to be a layman's guide to understanding biblical prophecy, contains a number of subjects written by 17 biblical scholars. These studies will help the reader to sort through conflicting claims and counter claims of biblical prophecy.

Clouse, Robert G. (editor). *The Meaning of the Millennium.* Downers Grove: InterVarsity Press, 1977.

This book contains discussion of the major views of the millennium, each view is presented by an able proponent. Each view is then criticized by those holding a different position. This book brings together the major views of the millennium, and their major strengths and weaknesses.

Cox, William E. *Amillennialism Today.* Philadelphia: Presbyterian and Reformed Publishing Co., 1972.

The author, holding to an amillennial view, discusses the biblical teachings relating to the endtimes. The author also includes a chapter in his study of a brief history of amillennialism as well as a chapter on principles of interpretation.

Guardini, Romano. *The Last Things.* Trans. by Charlotte E. Forsyth and Grace B. Branham. New York: Pantheon Books Inc., 1954.

This study of the Bible's teaching of last things is written from a Roman Catholic viewpoint. The book is written for the lay person.

Hughes, Phillip E. *Interpreting Prophecy.* Grand Rapids: Wm. B. Eerdmans Publishing Co., 1976.

This book is an excellent treatment on understanding biblical prophecy from a non-technical viewpoint. The author deals effectively with the language of prophecy and how it is to be understood.

Inch, Morris A. *Understanding Bible Prophecy.* New York: Harper and Row, Publishers, 1977.

The author discusses various aspects of biblical prophecy and comes to see it is a "living encounter between God and humanity." The author presents a solid biblical study of prophecy in non-technical language. A good treatment of an often misunderstood subject.

Katterjohn, Arthur and Mark Fackler. *The Tribulation People.* Carol Stream, Ill.: Creation House, 1975.

It is the authors' thesis the Christian will not be raptured before the great tribulation, but rather live through it bearing witness to Jesus Christ. The authors deal with the relevant Scripture texts relating to this subject.

Ladd, George Eldon. *The Last Things.* Grand Rapids: Wm. B. Eerdmans Publishing Co., 1978.

The author writes from a historic premillennial view as he discusses what the Bible says about the last things. This is one of the better books on eschatology from a premillennial view.

Miladin, George C. *Is This Really the End?* Cherry Hill, N.J.: Mack Publishing Company, 1972.

The author evaluates Hal Lindsey's book, *The Late Great Planet Earth*, and finds that there are major weaknesses in Lindsey's treatment of Holy Scripture. The book is only 55 pages long but there is much food for thought.

Morris, Leon. *Apocalyptic.* Grand Rapids: Wm. B. Eerdmans Publishing Co., 1977.

This little book deals with the nature and purpose of apocalyptic. It is written for the average person who wants to know more about this little understood part of the biblical background.

Payne, J. Barton. *Biblical Prophecy for Today.* Grand Rapids: Baker Book House, 1978.

The author writes from a premillennial view and focuses on the prophecies that Scripture itself claims to be predictive.

Travis, Stephen. *The Jesus Hope.* Downers Grove: InterVarsity Press, 1976.

This book emphasizes the concept of hope as it relates to the second coming of Jesus. Study questions at the end of each chapter help the reader to interact with the biblical themes being presented.

Wood, Leon J. *The Bible & Future Events.* Grand Rapids: Zondervan Publishing House, 1973.

The author writes from a dispensational viewpoint as he discusses what the Bible has to say about the future. Discussion questions at the end of the chapters help the reader to respond and interact with the material.

Books for Pastors
(and others interested in doing some in-depth study)

Beasley-Murray, G. R. *Jesus and the Future.* New York: St. Martins Press, 1954.

The author critically examines Jesus' teaching in Mark 13 from a historical and biblical perspective. The book is not easy reading, but much can be gained from a study of this kind.

Buis, Harry. The Doctrine of Eternal Punishment. Philadelphia: Presbyterian and Reformed Publishing Company, 1957.

The author deals with the subject of hell. He surveys this doctrine historically as it was taught in the Christian church. He deals with the present-day denials of hell and answers the objections presented.

Erickson, Millard J. *Contemporary Options in Eschatology. A Study of the Millennium.* Grand Rapids: Baker Book House, 1977.

The author has written a book that deals with the basic eschatological view preached in the church. He discusses the historical background of each view and then looks at each view's strength and weakness. This book is a good overview of the major eschatological systems.

Hoekema, Anthony A. *The Bible and the Future.* Grand Rapids: William B. Eerdmans Publishing Co., 1979.

This book may be the best book in print, at this time, of the Bible's teaching on eschatology from an amillennial perspective. The author's position is one of "inaugurated eschatology" and he establishes his position before discussing events of eschatology.

Kik, J. Marcellus. *An Eschatology of Victory.* Philadelphia: Presbyterian and Reformed Publishing Co., 1971.

This study of eschatology centers on Matthew 24 and Revelation 20. It is a study of biblical eschatology from a postmillennial perspective.

Ladd, George Eldon. *The Presence of the Future.* Grand Rapids: Wm. B. Eerdmans Publishing Co., 1973.

This book is a revised edition of the author's earlier work, *Jesus and the Kingdom.* The thesis of this book is that the kingdom of God involves two great movements, fulfillment within history, and consummation at the end of history. This is an excellent treatment of Jesus' teaching regarding the kingdom of God.

MacPherson, Dave. *The Incredible Cover-Up.* Plainfield, N.J.: Logos International, 1976.

The author, a news reporter, details his search for the origins of the pretribulation rapture teaching. His conclusions are that the pretribulation rapture teaching can be dated to the early 1800s and that they are not rooted in Scripture. The author raises some challenging questions that can no longer be sidestepped.

Pentecost, J. Dwight. *Things to Come.* Grand Rapids: Zondervan Publishing House, 1958.

A study in biblical eschatology from a premillennial dispensational perspective. The author deals with a mixture of subjects covering the whole range of eschatology.

Glossary

amillennialism: This view of the millennium does not deny the reality of the millennium but only that there is no sufficient ground for the expectation of a literal thousand-year period of time. This view holds that the teaching of the New Testament does not teach that the millennium will follow the Lord's coming, for the second advent immediately ushers in the final judgment and the eternal state. Amillennialism understands that the thousand years is a numerical symbol of a long but indefinite period of time extending from Jesus' ascension to his return (cf. 2 Peter 3:3–13).

antichrist: This word portrays the personification of all evil. This person opposes everything relative to God. He will, indeed, set himself up as God, in every sense being antichrist. But, in the end he will be destroyed by Christ (2 Thess. 2:8; Rev. 19:20–21).

armageddon: *"Har-Magedon"* is the Greek form of the Hebrew *Har-Meghiddo,* "Mount of Megiddo." It is found in the New Testament as "Armageddon" (Rev. 16:16). This mountain overlooks the plain of Esdraelon. In this large level plain numerous battles were fought (Judg. 5:19; 2 Kings 23:29; 2 Chron. 35:22). In Revelation 16:13–16 is recorded the gathering together at Armageddon the armies of those opposing Christ for the final battle of the ages. This battle is described in Revelation 19:11-21. These passages in Revelation speak in powerful symbolic language that Christ's victory is won not by material weapons, but with the spiritual weapon—the sword of the Spirit which is the Word of God. The truth proclaimed is that of the final and complete victory of Christ over all who oppose him (cf. Rev. 20:7-10).

apocalyptic: This word is derived from the Greek word *apokalypsis* (Rev. 1:1) which means "uncovering," or "revelation." Apocalyptic refers then to a type of writing or literature, that seeks to reveal what has been hidden. This literature uses much symbolic language and those who interpret apocalyptic must recognize the function of symbols in language.

consistent eschatology: This view of eschatology teaches that we can understand the person and work of Jesus only in terms of an apocalyptic worldview. His message was centered around the approaching end of the world and the meaning of Jesus' life is to be seen from this viewpoint.

consummation: This term refers to the act of completing or bringing to fulfillment. In reference to eschatology it would mean the completion of the process of redemption to which God has committed himself.

dispensationalism: This view of the millennium proclaims a thousand-year reign of peace following the second advent of our Lord. During this thousand-year reign God will bring to fulfillment all of the Old Testament promises to David and Abraham. National Israel will be restored, Christ will reign from Jerusalem, a Temple will be rebuilt and sacrifices reinstituted, and the nations of the world will be under Christ's rule. The Christian church has no place in this view since the church has been raptured from the earth. This view is defended in the notes of the *Scofield Reference Bible* and has been popularized by Hal Lindsey, *The Late Great Planet Earth*.

eschatology:	This word means the teaching of last things. It relates to the various elements or events concerning the return of Jesus Christ and the end of the age. While Jesus used eschatological language in much of his teaching, his major eschatological teaching is found in Matthew 24 and 25 (see the parallels in Mark 13 and Luke 21:5–36). It is to be noted that Jesus was answering three basic questions: the fall of Jerusalem; the second coming; the end of the age (Matt. 24:3).
eschaton:	This term would refer to the future age, the age to come.
idealized eschatology:	This view of eschatology teaches that such things as resurrection from the dead, the second coming of Christ, and the final judgment are not events occurring at the end of history. They are however, events that take place in history in the lives of people and in the course of history. Thus, each generation is faced with eschatological events to which they must respond.
inaugurated eschatology:	Those who hold this view of eschatology believe that the last days have begun in the life, death, and resurrection of Jesus Christ. The entire scope of biblical salvation, justification, regeneration, eternal life, is eschatological. The kingdom of God has come in the person and work of Jesus Christ. However, there are still certain events yet to take place; the return of Jesus Christ in power and glory, the resurrection of the dead, and the final destruction of death and evil. There is a present inaugurated eschatology but there is also a future of real events in which history will be ended and eternity will begin.
intermediate state:	This refers to the interval between one's death and the final resurrection. It is not a time of soul sleeping or an unconscious state (Matt. 22:31–32; Luke 16:22–26; Rev. 7:9–17). The hope of the Christian is not the joy and bliss of the intermediate state but the resurrection of the body (1 Cor. 15:35–57; Rom. 8:22–25).

A Little Season: This phrase describes a short period of time in which the lawless one (Satan) is loosed. (2 Thess. 2:8; Rev. 20:3b). This period would be a time of testing and refining for God's people. This period will be an intensification of evil and apostasy and will precede the second coming of our Lord.

millennium: This term refers to the "thousand years" mentioned in Revelation 20:2-5, 7. Different understandings of the millennium occur depending on whether or not one understands the "thousand years" literally or symbolically. Those who understand it literally will see a thousand-year reign of peace and prosperity either before Christ's return (postmillennialism) or after Christ's return (premillennialism and dispensationalism). Those who understand the "thousand years" symbolically will see it as a real period of time extending from Christ's first advent to his return (amillennialism), the duration of it known only to God.

parousia: This word, in its Greek form, is used 24 times in the New Testament. Its basic meaning is "coming" and from its New Testament usage it is evident that its principal use is with reference to the Lord's return.

postmillennialism: This view of the millennium sees a triumph of the church through an outpouring of the Holy Spirit and the preaching of Christ. Following this thousand-year reign of peace and prosperity on earth Christ will return.

posttribulation: Those who hold to a posttribulation teaching believe that Christians and the Church will go through the great tribulation and that Jesus will return after this period of testing and persecution.

premillennialism: Those who hold to this teaching believe that Jesus Christ will return and then establish an earthly reign for a thousand years prior to the end of the age. This kingdom is the interim period between the return of Christ and the final judgment. It is to be a period of peace and prosperity for the church. A recent form of this view is called "dispensationalism."

pretribulationism: This term describes the teaching that states that the church and the followers of Christ will not experience the "great tribulation." They will be raptured from the earth to meet Christ in the air and stay with him there until Christ returns to set up the millennial kingdom. The difference between "pre" and "post" tribulation is seen in relation to the church and whether or not one believes the church will go through the great tribulation.

purgatory: The teaching of a part of Christendom sets forth a place of temporal punishment in the intermediate state known as purgatory. It is taught that all those who die at peace with the church but who are not perfect must undergo penance and purifying suffering. The sufferings vary in intensity and duration and all suffering will terminate at the last judgment. Generally, Protestant faiths reject this teaching since the evidence on which this teaching is based is found not in the Bible, but in the Apocrypha, in 2 Maccabees 12:39–45.

rapture: This word has as a basic meaning "to seize, to snatch." This word is used to describe what takes place to Christians who are living at Jesus' return (1 Thess. 4:17). When the dead are raised, the living Christians will be "caught up" (raptured) together with them in the clouds to meet the Lord. Christians differ as to when this will take place, before or after the tribulation.

realized eschatology: This phrase describes the viewpoint of eschatology that teaches that the kingdom of God comes in the life, ministry, death and resurrection of Jesus Christ. In a real sense the hour of fulfillment is come. There is little, if any, reference to a future series of events that bring in the eternal state.

Satan bound: The reference to the binding of Satan is found in Revelation 20:1–2. The purpose of this binding is to keep Satan from "deceiving the nations any more until the thousand years were ended" (Rev. 20:3 NIV). Some Christians believe that this binding takes place when Christ returns to set up the millennial kingdom. However, a growing number of Bible students believe that this "binding of Satan" occurred in the life and ministry of Jesus (Matt. 12:29; Mark 3:23–27; Luke 10:17–19; John 12:20–32). The "binding of Satan" would then refer to Satan's inability to prevent the extension of the church by means of an active missionary program and that he is unable to destroy the church as a mighty missionary institution.

Satan released: This term refers to that short period of time just prior to Christ's return when Satan masses the forces of evil in one last all-out attempt to defeat and destroy the people of God.

Sheol/Hades: Hades is Greek for the abode or realm of the dead, corresponding to Sheol in the Old Testament. Hades/Sheol is not used in the sense of the final state of the wicked.

tribulation: The word "tribulation" has a basic meaning of being in a tight spot with seemingly no way out. Jesus used this word to describe the trials through which his followers would pass in spreading the gospel (John 16:33). He also referred to a "great tribulation" attending the fall of Jerusalem in A.D. 70. (Matt. 24:21). Some Christians see a period of "great tribulation" shortly before the end of the age.